YORK NOTES

The Winter's Tale

William Shakespeare

Notes by Lynn and Jeff Wood

D0231732

 Longman   York Press

YORK PRESS
322 Old Brompton Road, London SW5 9JH

PEARSON EDUCATION LIMITED
Edinburgh Gate, Harlow,
Essex CM20 2JE, United Kingdom
Associated companies, branches and representatives throughout the world

First published 1999
Thirteenth impression 2010

ISBN: 978-0-582-41474-7

Designed by Vicki Pacey
Phototypeset by Gem Graphics, Trenance, Mawgan Porth, Cornwall
Colour reproduction and film output by Spectrum Colour
Produced by Pearson Education Asia Limited, Hong Kong

CONTENTS

PART ONE

INTRODUCTION

HOW TO STUDY A PLAY

Studying a play on your own requires self-discipline and a carefully thought-out work plan in order to be effective.

- If you are coming to *The Winter's Tale* for the first time, it is essential to experience and enjoy it as a dramatic experience a few times before reading the play, embarking upon close textual analysis and, finally, developing your own critical reading. Shakespeare does not come readily off the page; listening to a performance is the most rewarding way of familiarising yourself with Shakespeare's language, hearing the variety of dramatic voices he uses and understanding the play's structure. Of the productions available on audio cassette, we recommend the recording of Peter Wood's 1961 production with John Gielgud as Leontes and Peggy Ashcroft as Paulina (Harper Collins ISBN 0001031481).

- Once you know the play well, the best way to develop a critical understanding of it is to explore some of Shakespeare's other plays with which it has most in common. Of the great **tragedies**, *Othello* (1604) and *King Lear* (1605) offer many interesting points of contrast. For example, do you agree with Bernard Shaw that Leontes's jealousy is far more convincing than Othello's? Is it true that Leontes is like a Lear given a second chance? As one of the late plays, *The Winter's Tale* has fascinating similarities to and striking differences from *The Tempest* (1611).

- Drama is a special kind of writing (the technical term is **genre**) because it needs a performance in the theatre to arrive at a full interpretation of its meaning. Try to imagine that you are a member of the audience when reading the play. Think about how it could be presented on the stage, not just about the words on the page.

- Drama is always about conflict of some sort (which may be below the surface). Identify the conflicts in the play and you will be close to identifying the large ideas or themes which bind all the parts together.

- Make careful notes on themes, character, plot and any sub-plots of the play.
- Why do you like or dislike the characters in the play? How do your feelings towards them develop and change?
- Playwrights find non-realistic ways of allowing an audience to see into the minds and motives of their characters, for example soliloquy, aside or music. Consider how such dramatic devices are used in the play you are studying.
- Think of the playwright writing the play. Why were these particular arrangements of events, characters and speeches chosen?
- Cite exact sources for all quotations, whether from the text itself or from critical commentaries. Wherever possible find your own examples from the play to back up your opinions.
- Always express your ideas in your own words.

This York Note offers an introduction to *The Winter's Tale* and cannot substitute for close reading of the text and the discriminating study of secondary sources.

READING *THE WINTER'S TALE*

In the final phase of their creative lives, some great artists stride into brave new worlds. The final group of plays by Shakespeare, like the late quartets of Beethoven, have provoked intense controversy. For every critic who finds these works odd and ridiculous there are twenty who believe that they are among the summits of artistic achievement – not just of Shakespeare and Beethoven but of Western Art.

It is easy to see why there have been critical voices raised against *The Winter's Tale* (1610). It breaks dramatic rules and offends common sense. No doubt these things help to explain the play's enormous continuing popularity.

Shakespeare's younger and more pretentious contemporary, Ben Jonson, believed that tragicomedy was the highest form of drama. As far as we know, Shakespeare didn't go in for polemics and in *Hamlet* (1601) he makes fun of pedants who try to squeeze plays into pigeon-holes. But *The Winter's Tale* is a tragicomedy and as such is like a summing up of Shakespeare's development as a poetic dramatist.

Shakespeare's art never stood still. Like Beethoven, he was a tireless experimenter, forever pushing forward, expanding the resources of poetic drama. To read again one of his earliest successes, the solemn bloodbath which is *Titus Andronicus* (1593), and then turn to *The Winter's Tale*, written twenty years later, is to gauge the extraordinary progress his craft made. It is not simply that the later play is much more skilfully constructed, the poetry richer and more flexible, the characterisation more engaging and more varied and the range of thought and feeling the play explores much more interesting because the characters and their problems are closer to everyday experience. The play inhabits a different world. It is the product of a different sensibility. Melodramatic gloom and inexplicable cruelty have given way to something more serious: an investigation of how real people's minds work and where people fit into the scheme of things. What's most striking is Shakespeare's dramatisation of faith. Particularly faith in young people.

In *The Winter's Tale*, we are invited to take a leap into the dark. Working experimentally, risking everything to find expression for what is almost beyond expression, Shakespeare offers us a way of observing and understanding people which requires imagination and flexibility of response on the part of the audience.

To begin with, we are given Shakespeare's most concentrated, most disciplined version of what tragedy is about. There are no histrionics; just a steady-eyed observation of the ways a person can damage himself and those about him for no good reason. Some people believe *Othello* (1604) is a tragedy about jealousy. *The Winter's Tale* makes what happens in the earlier play look more like melodrama. In technical terms, the advance in technique is simple. Leontes persuades *himself* that his wife is having an affair with his oldest, closest friend. There is no villain feeding him lies (as Iago does Othello); jealousy feeds upon itself to bring about its dangerous dislocations. The intensity of Leontes's mental turmoil is sharply etched. As we watch him all but destroy himself, we are made aware of the terrible fragility of everyone and everything valuable about him: his family and his kingdom. There are no wicked characters in *The Winter's Tale*. If Shakespeare's last plays have a philosophy, it is that evil is blindness, incomplete knowledge, self-delusion, not something brewed by devils. It is a notion of tragic suffering which Shakespeare had been developing from *Titus Andronicus* (1593), through *Hamlet* (1601) and *King Lear* (1605) and *Macbeth* (1606) but which is most clearly articulated in this play. One of the people involved in the rumpus observes, '… I am sure 'tis safer to / Avoid what's grown than question how 'tis born' (I.2.432–3). In fact, there is plenty for those interested in the psychology of jealousy to engage with in the opening scenes. But Camillo's words show us where the focus falls in Acts I–III: on the hideous self-inflicted pain of Leontes's obsession:

> Is whispering nothing?
> Is leaning cheek to cheek? Is meeting noses?
> Kissing with the inside lip? Stopping the career
> Of laughter with a sigh? – a note infallible
> Of breaking honesty. Horsing foot on foot?
> Skulking in corners? (I.2.284–9)

Dismissive descriptions of *The Winter's Tale* as something from the land of fairy tales, must be dealing either with an expurgated version of Shakespeare's play or with the serious fairy tales Angela Carter writes (for example, *The Bloody Chamber and Other Stories*, Gollancz, 1979). This is the clearest realisation of the tragic formula Shakespeare was working towards all his life. The answer to those lurid rhetorical questions Leontes has asked himself is the emphatic 'Yes!' he cannot, will not hear. Maybe such acute suffering is a kind of luxurious indulgence. When the awful cost of his emotional bout is revealed, Leontes's return to the flat, real world is as sudden as his descent into madness was precipitous: 'I have too much believed mine own suspicion' (III.2.149). This is what tragedy means. Pointless waste on a colossal scale. But then we ask with T.S. Eliot's Gerontion, 'After such knowledge, what forgiveness?' (see *Gerontion*, Hogarth Press, 1920). What happens in the world when people acknowledge the terrible things they have done to themselves and their families? Which is where the comic view of life comes sweeping in. One of the problems for the student approaching a 'tragicomedy' is that s/he may use the word 'comedy' differently from the way literary critics use it. Ben Jonson's view of things was based on the sane recognition that human life is an uneven compound of good things and bad. That if destruction is a fact of life, so is reconstruction. Things come and go and come again and again. The sense of comedy is intimately tied up with our experience of being in the world, with the experience of the seasons. Comedy is the energetic triumph of life over death, the affirmation of truth and vitality in the face of delusion and murder. Tragedy is not a more grown up way of seeing the world than comedy. It is limited and the balance is probably wrong. After all, winter occupies only one quarter of the year.

Because it is through the rhythms of the seasons, the experience of the family rather than through the linear womb-to-tomb progress which is the individual's perception of life that this vision of the real world, the spirit of comedy, is generated. Comedy *is* about 'laughter' (a potent word in the dark moments of Act II Scene 1). But that does not mean it is lightweight or trivial. What is wonderful and convincing about *The Winter's Tale* is its comic weight. Against the exquisite agony of the first part of the play, Shakespeare counterpoises his most robust picture of life. Act IV Scene 4 is without parallel in Shakespeare's dramatic output. Something of its richness is explored in the commentaries which follow but it would require a much larger volume than this one to begin to do it justice. What emerges from it in the theatre is the delight in love, in community, fellowship, 'the complete consort dancing together' (T.S. Eliot *Little Gidding*, Faber & Faber, 1944); the human comedy which incorporates a rogue and a goddess, a family crisis and a vision, common sense and intimations of the transcendent.

It is fitting that in trying to talk about this play, we keep reaching for the words of another poet working at the margin of what can be made intelligible. Shakespeare's method is more practical than Eliot's. He achieves what the later poet could only theorise about:

> where every word is at home
> Taking its place to support the others,
> The words neither diffident nor ostentatious,
> An easy commerce of the old and the new,
> The common word exact without vulgarity,
> The formal word precise but not pedantic
> (T.S. Eliot, *Little Gidding*, 1944, lines 217–22)

Shakespeare has the bold confidence to use, alternately and in all sorts of combinations, common talk and language charged with **symbolism**. It's achieved in this play with an easiness which is the fruit of a long practical apprenticeship. His audience has always been a challenging compound of the 'headpiece[s] extraordinary' which clustered about the Courts of Elizabeth and James I and the 'Lower messes' (I.2.227): the rest of us who must approach the sublime through the sensual apprehension of the grotesque in those tortured lines of Leontes quoted above and in the compensating picture of loveliness voiced by Florizel:

> What you do
> Still betters what is done. When you speak, sweet,
> I'd have you do it ever. When you sing,
> I'd have you buy and sell so, so give alms,
> Pray so, and, for the ord'ring your affairs,
> To sing them too. When you do dance, I wish you
> A wave o'th' sea, that you might ever do
> Nothing but that, move still, still so,
> And own no other function. Each your doing,
> So singular in each particular,
> Crowns what you are doing, in the present deeds,
> That all your acts are queens. (IV.4.135–46)

PART TWO

SUMMARIES & COMMENTARIES

We have none of Shakespeare's manuscripts. *The Winter's Tale* is one of the plays which has come down to us in only one version: that published after Shakespeare's death in *The First Folio* of 1623. The text has been carefully prepared for the reader (there are few useful stage directions) and the play has been effectively divided into acts and scenes, probably not by Shakespeare.

A facsimile of the First Folio text of *The Winter's Tale*, edited with an introduction by John Dover Wilson, is published by Faber and Gwyer (1929). There are many editions of *The Winter's Tale* generally available, which contain a stimulating variety of introductory essays and critical appendices. We particularly recommend the following: *The New Clarendon Shakespeare*, edited by S.L. Bethell (1956); *The Signet Classic Shakespeare*, edited by Frank Kermode (1963); *The Arden Edition*, edited by J.H.P. Pafford (1963); *The New Penguin Shakespeare*, edited by Ernest Schanzer (1969). Of recent editions of the play, the most user-friendly is *The Cambridge Schools Shakespeare*, edited by Sheila Innes and Elizabeth Huddlestone (1998). Its text is based on *The New Cambridge Shakespeare*, edited by Susan Snyder (1999). Also of considerable interest is *The Oxford Shakespeare*, edited by Stephen Orgel (1996). This Note is based on *The New Penguin Shakespeare* edition, edited by Ernest Schanzer (1969). All emphases in the quotes are our own.

SYNOPSIS

For nine months, Polixenes, the King of Bohemia, has been the guest of Leontes, King of Sicilia. Leontes's closest friend since childhood, he has been lavishly entertained. When Polixenes announces his intention to leave, Leontes pressurises him to stay and, met by his friend's determination to return home, instructs his heavily pregnant wife, Hermione, to dissuade his friend from leaving. She succeeds and Leontes erupts with jealousy. He convinces himself that Polixenes and Hermione are lovers and that the child about to be born is their bastard. He orders his principal courtier, Camillo, to poison his friend. Incredulous but unable to make Leontes see reason, the honest Camillo helps Polixenes escape.

The flight of Camillo and Polixenes convinces Leontes not only that his wife is an adulterer but that she is part of a conspiracy to have him murdered. He sends her to prison where she gives birth to a daughter. A lady of the court, Paulina, takes the child from the prison and presents it to the furious King, asserting that he, not Polixenes, is the father. Locked in his jealous delusions, Leontes commands Paulina's husband to take the infant to some remote place and abandon it to Chance. Meanwhile, Leontes proceeds to put Hermione on trial. He has dispatched servants to consult the Oracle which he has no doubt will confirm the Queen's guilt.

When the Oracle proclaims Leontes to be a jealous tyrant, the King denounces the Oracle. Immediately, his son is struck down and Hermione suffers a deathly faint. Leontes is shaken out of his grotesque folly and begs forgiveness, but Paulina announces that not only his son but also his wife are dead. The kingdom will be without an heir unless his lost daughter is recovered. Leontes begins long years of penance.

Meanwhile we see Paulina's husband, guided by a dream, leave the child in Bohemia, believing Polixenes to be the father. He and the crew of his ship suffer terrible deaths, but suddenly the mood of the play changes. A homely, charitable Shepherd and his son discover the child and a quantity of gold left with her. The baby is in safe hands.

Sixteen years pass. Leontes's lost daughter, Perdita, has grown up, a remarkable shepherdess with whom Florizel, Polixenes's son, has fallen in love. Against the jollity of a sheep-shearing festival, rich with music and dancing, disguised, his father and Camillo spy on the ardent young lovers. As they are about to be betrothed, Polixenes throws off his disguise and vents his fury on the son who dares marry so lowly a girl and without his father's approval. Camillo, who longs to see Leontes again, contrives the young couple's elopement to Sicilia then, revealing to Polixenes where they have gone, follows with the outraged King in pursuit. The Shepherd and his son, in fear of their lives attempt to tell Polixenes about Perdita's origins but are tricked aboard Florizel's ship and everyone reaches Sicilia without the truth's being discovered.

Meanwhile, sixteen years on, Leontes is still Paulina's humble penitent. Overjoyed at the unexpected arrival of Florizel and Perdita, when news comes that Polixenes and Camillo have pursued them to his kingdom, Leontes undertakes to speak on their behalf. To universal rejoicing, Camillo and his master, the two Kings, and Perdita and Leontes are reunited; the Shepherd and his son are incorporated into the royal family. Together they visit Paulina's house to view the remarkable statue of Hermione. In awe they see the 'statue' come to life: the Oracle's words fulfilled, Hermione can live again.

The play closes on a note of sublime wonder and joy.

ACT **I**

SCENE **1**   **Two courtiers paint a glowing picture of the friendship between Leontes, King of Sicilia, and Polixenes, King of Bohemia**

The action starts in the court of Leontes, King of Sicilia. Polixenes, King of Bohemia, his friend since childhood, has been staying with him. Two lords, Archidamus from Bohemia and Camillo from Sicilia, are discussing Leontes's lavish entertainment of his friend. Archidamus doubts that when Leontes visits Bohemia, they will be able to match Leontes's extraordinary generosity. Camillo explains that Leontes is so devoted to Polixenes that he cannot do enough for him. The Kings' friendship is so strong, nothing can threaten it. Brought up together as children, the Kings have sustained their love for one another whilst ruling their geographically remote kingdoms by exchanges of letters and gifts. Archidamus praises Leontes's young son, Prince Mamillius. Camillo confirms that he brings joy to the people of Sicilia and great things are expected of him.

> Like many of Shakespeare's opening scenes, this one begins in the middle of a conversation. An apparently lightweight dialogue of just 44 lines introduces themes which will shape the entire action of the play. The illusion of prosperity generated

by this elegant, slightly artificial chat contains the seeds of the catastrophe which will bring the first part of the drama to a tragic end.

Archidamus and Camillo exchange pleasantries but their pauses make the conversation sound strained. Their **prose** is not simply courtly but full of **hyperbole**: 'our entertainment shall shame us' (lines 8–9), 'such magnificence', 'so rare' 'I know not what to say' (lines 12–13). They talk about friendship but their language suggests competition. Stressing that Leontes's hospitality is 'given freely' (line 17), Camillo uses the vocabulary of commercial transactions: 'owes', 'pay', 'too dear' (lines 7–17).

Camillo paints a picture of their friendship so extravagant: 'they have seemed to be together … of opposed winds' (lines 28–30) that the audience anticipates a rupture. The word 'seemed' foreshadows the reality: all is not as perfect as it appears. When Camillo says that the friendship 'rooted betwixt them … cannot choose but *branch* now' (lines 23–4) he means 'flourish'. What we see all too soon is division and separation. There are further ironies in this brief exchange. Archidamus is correct in believing that there is not '*in the world* either malice or matter' (line 32) to alter the Kings' love: we will see the **tragedy** spring entirely from Leontes's 'weak-hinged fancy' (II.3.118).

By the end of Scene 2 we shall witness 'great difference' (i.e. hatred) between the Kings, Bohemia and Sicilia. And by the end of the play, the audience will have visited two very *different* kingdoms. For the theatre audience, the experience of Acts I, II, III and V is of a closed, courtly setting, in Act IV of a vibrantly contrasting, open-air, **pastoral** one.

Mention of the Kings' infancy and of Prince Mamillius introduces the theme of childhood and prepares the audience for the part that the young will play in paying for and then rectifying the mistakes of the old. The emphasis on Mamillius's healthy influence and potential is ironic and poignant when we know what will happen to him. His simple innocence will fail to 'physic' his father, but paradoxically it will be by his son's death that Leontes's lunacy will be punished and cured. The phrase 'physics the subject' (line 37) is the first of many images of disease cured which will colour the whole play.

The playful banter which ends the scene is also ominous. All this apparent prosperity is about to be swept violently aside. Shortly, the King will have 'no son' (line 43), the kingdom no heir; the King's distressed subjects will have to wait for sixteen years before gaining another in the shape of Leontes's son-in-law, Florizel, the son of Polixenes.

1 **Archidamus** this is the only time this Bohemian lord appears in the play. By the end of Act I, Camillo has become Polixenes's sole counsellor

Chance dramatic irony. Camillo will 'chance' to visit Bohemia much sooner than he expects; he will stay for sixteen years

4 **Bohemia and ... Sicilia** in this play, the words refer both to the countries they rule and to the kings themselves. Shakespeare takes the names of the two kingdoms straight from Robert Greene's *Pandosto* (1588) but transposes events, the action beginning in Sicilia. In the play, Bohemia (the present day Czech Republic) retains its coastline in the face of geographical fact and Ben Jonson's sniping

14 **insufficience** shortcomings

24 **branch** wordplay – (a) flourish (b) diverge

27 **royally attorneyed** lavishly compensated for

37 **physics the subject** makes everyone feel healthy, acts as a general tonic

SCENE 2   King Polixenes announces his departure. King Leontes is seized with a jealous conviction that Polixenes is the father of his pregnant Queen's child. He orders Camillo to poison Polixenes. Camillo and Polixenes flee the country

This scene consists of three linked episodes:
1 Polixenes thanks Leontes profusely for his nine months' hospitality. Fearing what may happen in Bohemia in his absence, he announces he will depart next day. Four times, Leontes begs his friend to stay. Met with Polixenes's determination to leave, he prompts Hermione to use her eloquence. The Queen reassures Polixenes that all is well in Bohemia and promises that if he'll stay a week longer, she will allow

Leontes to stay an extra month when he returns the visit. When all else fails, playfully, she boxes Polixenes into a position where he has no choice but to remain: either as her guest or as her prisoner. Graciously, he gives in.

Whilst Leontes's attention is elsewhere, Hermione questions Polixenes about his and Leontes's boyhood. When Leontes discovers that Hermione has succeeded in persuading Polixenes to stay where he had failed, instead of sounding pleased, he seems hurt. He compares Hermione's success with Polixenes to the words she spoke when she vowed to be his wife. Misreading her husband's apparent approval of her charm offensive, Hermione takes Polixenes's hand and proclaims him her 'friend' (line 108). Whilst they chat, Leontes draws aside, suddenly revealing to the audience filthy suspicions about Polixenes and Hermione. Quickly, he convinces himself that they are lovers. His heady mood swings between violent jealous doubt as he watches them and desperate reassurance as he traces his own likeness in his son Mamillius's face.

Hermione and Polixenes sense that Leontes is 'unsettled' (line 147) . Leontes's explanation is that, stirred by looking at his son, he is moved by fond memories of his own childhood. Polixenes expresses a similar attachment to *his* son. Again, Leontes steps aside with Mamillius and, sinisterly, instructs Hermione, 'How thou lov'st us show in our brother's welcome' (line 174). Wholly innocent of Leontes's suspicions, Hermione and Polixenes go off into the garden.

2 Alone, and wild with jealousy, Leontes is convinced he is a cuckold. He sends Mamillius away and shares his thinking with the incredulous Camillo. Certain of his interpretation of events, deaf to reason, he tries to browbeat Camillo into seeing things the way he does and orders him to poison Polixenes. Realising that Leontes will not 'be cured / Of [his] diseased opinion' (lines 296–7) Camillo agrees to 'fetch off' (line 334) Polixenes on condition Leontes spare Hermione. Leontes departs, promising to 'seem friendly' (line 350).

3 Camillo shares his moral dilemma with the audience. Either he must disobey a King or murder one. He concludes that his duty is clear and he must 'Forsake the court' (line 362). Fortunately, Polixenes enters, and remarks on the marked change in Leontes's behaviour towards

him. Revealing the awful situation cautiously, step by step, Camillo explains to Polixenes the predicament the two of them are in. He convinces the horrified King that their lives are in jeopardy. The King entrusts Camillo to effect their escape. Unable to help her, Polixenes expresses his fears for Hermione's safety.

The mood of the play plunges precipitously in this scene: from apparent harmony and stability to division, madness and impending **tragedy**. The Camillo who eulogised Leontes's love for Polixenes in Act I Scene 1, just three hundred lines later finds himself commanded by the King to murder his life-long friend.

When we see the two kings for the first time, we see also the heavily pregnant Hermione and the engaging young Prince, Mamillius. The tragic movement of this scene is that all the feelings of hope and fruition which that **tableau** should promote are wilfully displaced by Leontes's mad, violent, causeless jealousy.

Some critics have suggested that Leontes's jealousy makes no psychological sense at all. But by a tragic irony, the opening words of Polixenes's courtly, rhetorical thank-you speech draw attention to a coincidence. 'Nine changes of the watery star' (line 1) measures both the length of his stay in Sicilia and the precise duration of Hermione's pregnancy. If Leontes is thinking at all, perhaps he suspects his friend's sudden desire to leave is connected with the imminent birth of Hermione's baby. This might be a better explanation of his stubborn determination to keep his guest there than simply a crazy possessiveness. Already, consciously or unconsciously, Leontes is on the track which leads to his ordering Camillo to poison the man he believes has betrayed him. Instead of heralding celebration and an increase in happiness, the unborn child has become the catalyst for a process ending in chaos and death.

As the scene unfolds (lines 1–25), Shakespeare contrasts sharply Polixenes's easy eloquence with his fellow-king's abrupt, clumsy responses. It is ironic that in calling for her assistance, Leontes should accuse his wife of being 'Tongue-tied' (line 27). The phrase describes himself perfectly. Hermione's manner is as light-hearted, witty, flowing and poised as Leontes's is preoccupied, sombre and awkward.

Interestingly, both Polixenes and Hermione are sensitive to Leontes's insecurity before it is revealed to us in his soliloquy. Perhaps it is habitual. Polixenes, unfortunately as it turns out, assures Leontes that: 'There is no tongue that moves, none, none i'th'world / So soon as yours could win me' (lines 20–1). Similarly, Hermione, bargaining with Polixenes for an extra week of his society in exchange for a month's of Leontes's, is quick to reassure her hypersensitive husband: 'yet ... Leontes, / I love thee not a jar o'th'clock behind / What lady she her lord' (lines 42–4).

Although the two Kings call each other 'brother' (lines 15, 27) and declare their affection for each other, Leontes is neither polite nor caring to Polixenes; he is not interested in what his friend wants to do, this pressuring friendship is, as Polixenes hints, more like 'a whip' (line 25). Their conversation is a battle of wills, a continuation of the competition and rivalry that sounded a false note in the opening scene. Leontes is brooding; he speaks in abrupt statements and commands, and when he is unable to engage in a reasonable conversation, he simply adopts a position 'I'll no gainsaying' (line 19). Having ordered Hermione to speak, he encourages her and then 'draws apart' to return some fifty lines later. He misses therefore most of Hermione's and Polixenes's ensuing conversation.

As he rejoins the couple, the words he may overhear, 'If you first sinn'd with us ... but us' (lines 84–6) could not be better calculated to madden an already insecure husband. This is why instead of being pleased with his wife's success in doing what he asked her to do, Leontes sounds offended 'At my request he would not' (line 87).

His gloomy account of his courtship of Hermione (lines 101–5) reveals what extraordinary distortions are taking place in his mind. By drawing a parallel between Hermione's success in persuading Polixenes to stay and her agreeing to marry *him*, he reveals that what seems to hurt him is the speed with which Hermione and Polixenes have come to agreement. The tempo of these lines is sluggish and laboured. The stresses which fall upon the unpleasant words 'three crabbèd months' and 'soured themselves to death' (line 102) capture his memory of their courtship as a period of protracted suffering and reveal his present bitterness. He reminds Hermione of that promise made so many years ago, 'then didst thou utter / "I am yours for ever"' (line 104), only to impress on the audience again his sense of having lost everything but a legal hold over her affections.

Unfortunately, Hermione's next comment includes the words 'husband' and 'friend' (lines 107–8) together. This antithesis and her gesture of giving Polixenes her lovely hand so soon after Leontes talking about her giving it to *him*, confirms Leontes's suspicions that he has been cuckolded. Feeling side-lined and out-performed, he convinces himself that what he sees next is evidence of the ultimate intimacy between his one time closest friends: 'Too hot, too hot' (line 108) and again, he draws aside to dwell on and elaborate his feelings.

In this scene, Leontes feels he has lost not only his wife but his closest friend. Their easy, courtly language makes his own sound childish by comparison. They talk like an adult couple and expose his lack of ease. In all innocence, his wife has publicly humiliated him by succeeding with that sophisticated banter he lacked to out-manoeuvre his old friend. It's not simply that it feels to him that Polixenes wants to stay for Hermione's sake rather than his, it is that he feels Polixenes *deserves* her. This explains his curious preoccupation with the past, fondly identifying with his young son and the time when he and Polixenes were partners. Leontes's troubled asides are the subject of Text 1 of Textual Analysis. The conversation which takes place between Hermione and Polixenes is discussed in the Theme on Children and Childhood.

The conversation between Camillo and Leontes (lines 212–350) is the first of several where a wholly disinterested, loyal subject tries to restore Leontes's clear sight. Leontes is now one 'Who, in rebellion with himself, will have / All that are his so too' (line 355). Their exchanges depend on what each of them 'perceives' and 'notes'. The process which began in Leontes's asides culminates two hundred lines later in a passage (lines 284–96) where thought is paralysed by its own heady wilfulness. Leontes's repeats the word 'nothing' nine times as his words crescendo towards the statement that 'nothing have these nothings / If this be nothing' (lines 295–6). Ironically Leontes's self-deception leaves Camillo no choice but to use deceit himself; it is the first of a number of incidents where, all else having failed, a character will be forced to deceive to good purpose.

However ludicrous Leontes's suspicions may seem, the conviction he feels and the pain it causes him are powerfully portrayed. Polixenes knows him well enough to appreciate the violence of his passion and there is something poignant about the fact that Leontes comes so near to the truth when he asks Camillo, 'Dost think I am so muddy, so unsettled, / To appoint my self in this vexation ... / ... Would I do this? / Could man so blench?' (lines 325–33). Shakespeare at once presents Leontes's jealousy as peculiarly his own and as that kind of self-inflicted madness to which everyone can fall victim.

1 **watery star** the moon

2 **the shepherd's note** the phrase anticipates the second part of the play which takes place in rural Bohemia

6–7 **like a cipher ... in rich place** as a digit can signify a large number

13 **sneaping** killing with cold

19 **I'll no gainsaying** I won't take no for an answer

19 **Press** a metaphor suggesting a common Elizabethan torture

30 **Charge him too coldly** don't use strong enough arguments

31–2 **this satisfaction / ... proclaimed** this was the news yesterday

33 **his best ward** his strongest line of defence

37 **distaffs** sticks used by women to hold the flax they spin into wool

38 **adventure** risk, invest

41 **gest** date

43–4 **I love thee ... / ... lord** I love you as much as any wife loves her husband

47 **limber** feeble

51 **potent** powerful

53–4 **pay your fees / ... thanks** in Shakespeare's time, prisoners had to pay the costs of being accommodated in gaol

57 **should import offending** would be bad manners

66 **the verier wag** the more mischievous

67 **lambs** another allusion linking the **pastoral** world of Bohemia to childhood

68 **changed** exchanged

70 **The doctrine of ill-doing** sin

72–3 **our weak spirits ... / ... with stronger blood** had we never matured physically

74–5 **the imposition ... / ... ours** Christian doctrine says that we all inherit original sin from Adam's disobedience of God. Polixenes's words could mean either a) apart from the sin we inherited, we were pure or b) our life was so faultless even our original sin had been purged

76 **tripped** sinned

78 **unfledged** immature

80–1 **Grace to boot! / ... conclusion** Heaven help us! Don't follow this line of argument to its logical conclusion

91–2 **Cram's with praise ... / ... things** Hermione is saying how warmly women respond to praise

92–3 **One good deed ... / ... upon that** without praise people are discouraged from doing more good things

94–6 **You may ride's / ... acre** unfortunately, by **metaphorically** comparing women to horses, Hermione introduces sexual **innuendos**. Leontes's jealous hypersensitivity no doubt registers this

99 **Grace** virtue (the opposite of being a devil)

104 **clap** promise

108 **friend** Leontes hears the word as meaning 'lover'

110 **tremor cordis** palpitations of the heart

112 **May a free face put on** may be innocent or may just *look* innocent

118 **The mort o'th'deer** the sigh a deer makes as it dies (again, the phrase has sexual overtones)

119 **my brows** from now on Leontes's imagination is haunted by the figure of himself as a ridiculous cuckold with horns sprouting from his temples

121 **bawcock** fine fellow (a term of endearment)

123 **neat** wordplay – a) clean b) horned like cattle

125 **virginalling** wordplay – a) like someone playing the virginals b) Leontes is quibbling with the idea of Hermione surrendering her chastity

126 **wanton** lively

128–9 **want'st ... / ... like me** to be really like me you would need a pair of horns

136 **welkin** clear, pure, healthy like the blue sky

137 **collop** piece of my flesh

137 **dam** mother (usually used of animals)

146 **hardening of my brows** another reference to his imaginary cuckold's horns

151 **Nature** human tenderness (like mine for my son)

153 **harder bosoms** Leontes is convincing himself that Hermione and Polixenes are brazen and dishonest

155 **unbreeched** in the sixteenth century little boys wore skirts not trousers

158 **as ornaments oft does** no doubt Leontes is thinking of Hermione

160 **squash** an unripe peapod

161 **Will you take eggs for money?** are you the sort of person who'll be fobbed off with something worthless?

168 **parasite** flatterer (here, a term of endearment)

186 **forked** another allusion to a cuckold's horns

188 **issue** a pun – a) offspring b) consequence

189 **Contempt ... / ... knell** when I die everyone will mock me

219 **gust it** realise

223–7 **any understanding pate ... / ... headpiece extraordinary** someone of superior intelligence

227 **Lower messes** ordinary, less acute people

228, **business ... satisfy ... mistress** Camillo innocently chooses precisely the
232–3 words to fuel Leontes's jealous fantasies

237 **chamber-counsels** intimate secrets

242 **bide upon** insist upon it

244 **hoxes honesty behind** the metaphor comes from the practice of deliberately hobbling cattle

246 **grafted** implanted

248 **played ... drawn** completed and the prize won

260–1 **Whereof ... / ... non-performance** that showed I'd failed in my duty

273 **slippery** unfaithful

276 **hobby-horse** whore

277 **rank** foul

277–8 **as any flax-wench / ... troth-plight** like a common country slut who surrenders her virginity before she's engaged

301 **gross lout, mindless slave** Leontes's language becomes increasingly puerile

306 **The running of one glass** an hour

314 **benched and reared to worship** promoted

318 **cordial** medicinal

333 **blench** go so terribly wrong

334 **fetch off** the words are carefully ambiguous – Leontes hears 'murder' but Camillo intends 'help escape'

341 **I'll give no ... none** a promise Leontes fails to keep

361 **Let villainy ... forswear't** even a villain would be mad to kill a King

378 **Be intelligent** tell me what you know

388 **basilisk** a mythical creature whose looks killed

392–4 **Clerk-like ... / ... gentle** Polixenes is praising Camillo as someone who has risen by merit not inheritance. The phrase 'clerk-like' also suggests the priestly role he plays as confessor to both Kings

400 **conjure** urge, command

419 **his that did betray the Best!** Judas

436 **impawned** pledged

441 **discovery** revelation

456 **Professed** claimed to be his friend

ACT II

SCENE 1   Hermione plays with Mamillius; Leontes accuses the Queen of adultery and treason and orders her to prison

This scene consists of three linked episodes:

1 Hermione and her ladies-in-waiting are playing with Prince Mamillius. Hermione is nearing the end of her pregnancy. The ladies and Mamillius tease each other. Hermione asks her son to tell them a tale. He begins to whisper a 'sad tale' to her as it is 'best for winter' (line 25).

2 Leontes enters. He has just learned of Polixenes's and Camillo's flight. The speed and secrecy of their departure convinces him that there is a conspiracy against him. He assumes that Camillo knew of the adultery and was Polixenes's and Hermione's go-between. He orders Mamillius to be taken away from Hermione. Surprised, she asks if this is a game. Leontes accuses Hermione publicly of adultery with Polixenes and, convinced she is in league with the King and Camillo to kill him, sends her to prison. Hermione protests her innocence firmly, quietly and with dignity; she tells her women to shed tears only if she's proven guilty and escapes prison. Trusting in Heaven, she determines to be

patient. She leaves, sad that her hope must be to see Leontes sorry for his false accusations.

3 As Camillo had done, Antigonus and a Lord try to persuade Leontes that Hermione is 'spotless' (line 131). They swear on their own and their families' lives that she is unblemished. Leontes won't listen; unable to support his accusations with evidence he asserts his power, 'Our prerogative / Calls not your counsels' (lines 163–4). Quite satisfied with his 'conjecture' (line 176), he has, however, sent messengers to Apollo's oracle at Delphos to confirm the truth of his accusations.

Following Polixenes's and Camillo's desperate departure, this scene highlights Hermione's vulnerability and traces her development into a tragic heroine of unparalleled dignity. As the scene opens, knowing what the Queen as yet has no inkling of, the audience feels the **pathos** of her situation. This is carefully augmented by Shakespeare's use of contrasting styles of language.

Where Leontes's behaviour with Mamillius in Act I Scene 2 disturbed the audience, the opening of this scene is moving for exactly the opposite reason. Hermione and the child relate naturally, tenderly to one another. In lines 1–31 we see Mamillius's engaging precocity most fully. It is his last appearance on stage. When Leontes enters, in those moments before his madness destroys everything, we are given again a tantalising glimpse of what might have been: a delightful family **tableau**, with Hermione's pregnancy promising even greater happiness to come.

But Mamillius's talk of 'Sprites and goblins' (line 26) anticipates the chilling impact Leontes's behaviour is about to have on them all. There is dramatic irony too. Like the man in the story, this King will dwell 'by a churchyard' (line 30), visiting daily his dead wife's tomb for the sixteen years of barren winter his crimes are about to usher in.

For the theatre audience, the dramatic tension rises as it continues to watch the innocent child and his mother quietly sharing their fantastic 'winter's tale' whilst hearing Leontes interrogating the anonymous Lord. The juxtaposition of the two actions is a powerful theatrical effect.

As Shakespeare moves towards the first climactic moment (Hermione's trial) Leontes's observations become, ironically, more coherently expressed. He sees every development as confirmation of his foul suspicions: 'All's true that is mistrusted' (line 48). At the same time, Shakespeare presents a united chorus of dissident voices ranged against him. His courtiers, like the loyal Queen and Camillo, are neither doormats nor sycophants. Their allegiance is equally to the King and to the truth. The moral design is not complicated as in Shakespeare's **tragedies** by the self-interest of a Iago (in *Othello*) or an Edmund (in *King Lear*).

Shakespeare gives Leontes at this point what is virtually a self-contained **metaphysical** poem of ugly power, clustered about one of the most disturbing images in the whole play: 'There may be in the cup / A spider steeped ... / ... I have drunk and seen the spider' (lines 39–45). It recalls Macbeth's vivid, graphic presentation of the torments of the damned: 'O full of scorpions is my mind' (*Macbeth*, III.2.36).

It is at this point in the development of Leontes's tragedy that the audience begins to feel some sympathy for the deranged King. If this were not the case, the tragic climax of Act Three would seem no more than wholly merited retribution. So when Leontes is perplexed by everyone else's inability to see what is as clear to him as a church by daylight, Shakespeare humanises him with a witty conceit: 'You smell this business with a sense as cold / As is a dead man's nose' (lines 151–2). In the midst of his heady career towards self-destruction, he stumbles upon the ironic truth which will shape the course of the next sixteen years of his life: 'The matter, / The loss, the gain, the ord'ring on't, is all / Properly ours' (lines 168–70). And as the scene progresses, the audience is given subliminally the first rays of hope; they become aware of a system of justice beyond anything Leontes controls. Hermione's understanding of her suffering as part of a divine plan: 'This action I now go on / Is for my better grace' (lines 121–2) is echoed and reinforced immediately by the courtier's assertion: 'the Queen is spotless / I'th'eyes of heaven' (lines 131–2). This coupled with Antigonus's insistent, earthy common-sense judgement: 'If it prove / ... otherwise ... / ... whole dungy earth' (lines 133–57) leads to a psychologically satisfying shift in Leontes's heady progress. His absolute 'right divine to govern wrong' uncompromised, he will submit to a higher authority: the Oracle. In his arrogance, Leontes's is certain that the Oracle will underwrite everything he has imagined but from the moment Apollo is mentioned, we can see that the tragedy will work within some kind of limit. The trouble is not yet over, the suffering not yet begun in earnest, but when this scene ends with Antigonus's wry observation that the business will raise them all 'To laughter ... / If the good truth were known' (lines 198–9), that curious word 'laughter' resonates. We are in a world where tragedy will not have the final say.

8 **Your brows are blacker** in Shakespeare's time fashionable beauty was blonde

18 **wanton** play

33 **train** attendants

35 **scour** run

44 **cracks his gorge** retches

46 **pander** acted as a go-between for Hermione and Polixenes

50 **discovered my design** betrayed my plans

51 **pinched** insignificant and tormented

58 **Sport** wordplay – Hermione asks if it's a joke. Leontes gives the word sexual overtones

68 **honest** sexually chaste

73 **calumny** gossip, slander

79 **replenished** complete

90 **fedary** accomplice

102 **centre** the whole world

122 **better grace** Hermione senses that she is being tested by God

135 **I'll go in couples with her** I won't let her out of my sight

141 **abused, and by some putter-on** deceived by some villain

143 **lam-damn** make him suffer

147 **geld** neuter

149 **glib myself** punish myself

161–4 **Why, what need we / ... counsels** Leontes is asserting the divine right of Kings to do whatever they like

177 **naught for approbation** lacking no proof

185 **of stuffed sufficiency** thoroughly competent

SCENE 2   **We meet 'that audacious lady' (III.3.42) Paulina. She visits the prison and collects Leontes's and Hermione's new-born daughter. She vows to confront the 'dangerous, unsafe lunes i'th'king' (line 30)**

This short episode is set in the prison where Hermione is being held. Antigonus's wife, Paulina, with her attendants come to visit her. Certain there are plots everywhere, Leontes has forbidden anyone access to the Queen. Paulina, alone, is allowed to speak to Emilia. We learn that Hermione has given birth to a daughter. Paulina offers to take the baby and present her to Leontes, hopeful that 'he may soften at the sight o'th'child' (line 40). Paulina wittily convinces the anxious gaoler that he has nothing to fear in allowing the child out.

> We see Paulina's power before we hear it: she strides onto the stage with an entourage. She inspires confidence by her utter fearlessness and conviction that the King is mad. Whilst Antigonus's final remark in the previous scene was an aside, we can tell from her first entry that Paulina will confront Leontes directly. Her energy and eloquence give us hope that she will succeed in persuading Leontes where everybody else has failed. Motivated entirely by her loyalty to the King and Queen and possessed of a common-sense contempt for fantasy, she has a bustling, shrewish, no nonsense abruptness which belies any idea that 'women in those days' lived under men's thumbs: 'Here's ado / To lock up honesty (lines 9–10) … 'Here's such ado' (line 19).

> The news of another child who is 'Lusty, and like to live' (line 27) injects a further note of hope and optimism. But this scene also brings home the reality and indignity of Leontes's harsh treatment of his Queen whose 'frights and griefs' (line 23) have made her give birth prematurely. This is the first of several episodes where Paulina

will act on behalf of speak for or about Hermione when she cannot speak for herself.

The witty argument Paulina uses to persuade the gaoler that he is doing what's right in letting the child out of prison again strengthens the feeling at this stage in the tragic movement that there is a far greater power in control of things than the tyrannous King's. The child is 'Freed and enfranchised' (line 61) 'By law and process of great Nature' (line 60).

19-20 **to make no stain ... / ... colouring** what a lot of energy has been expended to make someone who is wholly innocent seem thoroughly evil

32 **Becomes** suits

34 **red-looked anger** Paulina's preparing us for the bold outspoken way she will deal with Leontes

44-5 **cannot miss / A thriving issue** must succeed

49 **hammered of this design** thought of this plan

SCENE 3   **Leontes is restless; Mamillius is unwell. Paulina presents the King with his baby daughter. Furious, he orders Antigonus to take away the baby and abandon it. Cleomenes and Dion have returned with the Oracle's judgement. Leontes convenes the court to try Hermione**

This scene consists of four linked episodes

1 It is night time. Leontes is sleepless, tortured by the idea that, safe from his revenge, Polixenes and Camillo are laughing at him. But Hermione is within his grasp. Perhaps by killing her, he will find some relief. We hear that Mamillius is ill. Leontes's diagnosis is that the boy is sick with the shame of his mother's adultery.

2 Ignoring the courtiers' attempts to prevent her, Paulina enters Leontes's chamber, carrying his baby daughter. She proclaims her mission is to cure the King, to bring him 'sleep' (line 33). Leontes has been anticipating and dreading a visit from this 'audacious lady' (line 42). He taunts her husband Antigonus for not being able to 'rule her' (line 46) but the King has no more success, no matter how threatening his language becomes. Defiantly, Paulina insists to the

wild Leontes that his 'good queen' (line 58) has given birth to *his* baby daughter. She lays down the child before him. Leontes calls her a witch and a traitor; he orders her to leave, taking the 'bastard' (line 73) with her. Paulina refuses, insisting that by slandering his wife and children Leontes is a traitor to himself. Her strident tone modulates as tenderly she describes the princess whose baby features are so precisely a 'copy of the father' (line 99). Again, Leontes orders Paulina from the chamber and threatens to burn her at the stake. Undaunted, Paulina says that Leontes is little short of a tyrant since all his accusations depend only on his 'weak-hinged fancy'(line 118). Brushing aside the courtiers who try to manhandle her out of the room, Paulina departs of her own accord, leaving the baby princess at her father's feet.

3 Rattled, Leontes accuses Antigonus of setting his wife onto him. He orders him to take the baby away and 'see it instantly consumed with fire' (line 133). He threatens to kill him and his family if he disobeys; if Antigonus will not oblige, he will dash out 'The bastard brains' (line 139) himself. Supported by everyone else in the court, Antigonus denies responsibility for Paulina's visit and begs Leontes to abandon his cruel plan lest it have terrible consequences. Reluctantly, responding to the whole court's kneeling appeal, Leontes relents whilst insisting that the baby is 'a bastard' he'll not 'live on to see … kneel / And call [him] father' (lines 154–5). He commands Antigonus to convey the baby 'To some remote and desert place' (line 175) far from Sicily. With a heavy heart, Antigonus leaves with the child, wishing Leontes a prosperity greater than such a crime deserves.

4 News comes that Cleomenes and Dion have returned sooner than expected from Delphos. Excited and certain that the Oracle will confirm the Queen's guilt, Leontes summons a session to try Hermione.

We come upon a solitary Leontes tortured, like the guilty Macbeth, with insomnia. The three negatives with which the scene opens 'Nor night, nor day no rest!' (line 1) emphasise his despair; the **ostinato rhythm** of the words mimics his agitation. Trapped in and isolated by his delusions, his perceptions are distorted. Again, recalling Macbeth, Leontes sees it as 'weakness / … mere weakness' (lines 1–2) to allow Hermione to live. But as the scene develops we see that in spite of himself, Leontes's wildness is several measures short of blind mania. When, following Paulina's uncompromising administration of 'med'cinal' truth (line 37), Leontes is persuaded by Antigonus against burning the baby, the King describes himself as a 'feather for each wind that blows' (line 153), the image is reassuring; when it comes to the point, Paulina, the child and Antigonus are spared from the flames of immediate destruction. The sight of the baby rouses Leontes to passion and violence and although she escapes the flames, the child is committed to the mercy of Fortune. The visual impact of the baby's vulnerability juxtaposed with Leontes's savage threats serves once again to alienate the audience from the mad King.

Having slandered his wife, now he abuses his daughter calling her 'bastard' (line 73), 'brat' (line 92), 'it' (line 94). However, the entry of Paulina has succeeded in checking Leontes. Whilst they share the stage, (lines 27–129) she has four times as many lines as the King. Her common sense and the claims of natural justice ring out whilst Leontes is reduced to little more than abusive retorts and wild threats. The dramatic weight of things is shifting decisively against the King's lunacy. Like the uncompromising prophet in the wilderness, Paulina's words anticipate the Oracle's pronouncement in the following scene: Leontes is 'tyrannous' and 'jealous', his wife 'innocent' and 'free' (lines 28–30). Unwavering in her faith, Paulina insists that Hermione is a 'good' queen, trumpeting the word seven times. Although Leontes refuses to acknowledge the child, his silence as Paulina paints her pretty portrait of the baby (lines 97–107) could be played in many different ways. What is he doing while Paulina talks? Do we see someone torn between natural feeling and stubborn pride?

The sanity, selflessness and honesty of Paulina and Antigonus highlight the destructive, lonely egotism of Leontes and give the audience a picture of humanity in which there is much more to admire than despise. This is the last time Paulina and her husband see each other. Prophetically, Antigonus vows to 'pawn the little blood' (line 165) he has left to save the princess. In fearing that the child is 'condemned to loss' (line 191) and hoping that the wolves and bears might 'pity' (line 188) it, he anticipates his own hideous death. Yet, at the same moment, the phrase 'Where chance may nurse or end it' (line 182) opens up for the audience the possibility of survival and a happy resolution.

The scene ends on a positive note. Cleomenes and Dion have journeyed with 'good speed' (line 198) to and from Delphos. The phrase means both 'quickly' and 'successfully, propitiously'. Despite Leontes's promise to give Hermione a 'just and open trial' (line 204), he is prompted by his belief that she will be condemned by the Oracle and, ironically, that it will be her death which will bring him rest. As Act II draws to an end, the audience waits in quiet confidence that the king's diseased opinion is about to be cured.

4 **harlot-king** Leontes thinks of Polixenes as an adulterer

8 **a moiety** a little

18 **no thought of him!** again he is thinking of Polixenes

27 **be second to me** support me, back me up

30 **free** innocent

41 **gossips** godparents (for the baby)

49 **Commit me for committing honour** send me to prison for doing something decent

67 **A mankind witch!** a virago

68 **intelligencing bawd** now Leontes is accusing Paulina of being like Camillo, a go-between in the supposed love-affair between his wife and Polixenes

74 **dotard ... woman-tired, un-roosted** Leontes is accusing Antigonus of being a feeble, hen-pecked husband

90 **callat** a scold, a shrewish woman

93 **issue** child

104 **got it** fathered it

106 **yellow** the colour of jealousy

108 **losel** scoundrel, (directed at Antigonus)

109 **stay her tongue** shut her up

126 **What needs these hands?** an implied stage direction; the courtiers are attempting to shove Paulina from the chamber

139 **proper** own

152 **foul issue** terrible consequence

154-5 **Shall I live ... / ... father?** dramatic irony; this will happen in Act V

159 **Lady Margery** a variation of 'Dame Partlet the hen'

ACT III

SCENE 1   Leontes's agents are travelling back from Delphos

As Cleomenes and Dion approach Leontes's court, they pause to change horses and, for the benefit of the audience, reflect on their experiences at Delphos. They hope that the Oracle will prove as 'successful' (line 12) for Hermione by confirming her innocence, as the journey has been 'pleasant' and 'speedy' (line 13) for them.

> This refreshing episode comes between Leontes's summoning of Hermione's trial and the trial itself. Its twenty two lines are remarkable for the number of positive words they contain: 'delicate', 'most sweet / Fertile', 'celestial', 'successful', 'rare, pleasant, speedy', 'rare', 'fresh', 'gracious': in every way an uplifting contrast to the confined and harsh atmosphere of the Sicilian court.
>
> As Shakespeare prepares us for the climactic trial scene, we are made vividly aware of a reality transcending the world of Leontes and his 'proclamations / So forcing faults upon Hermione' (lines 15–16). We anticipate that the terrible supernatural voice, 'the ear-deaf'ning voice o'th'oracle, / Kin to Jove's thunder' (lines 9–10) is about to endorse everyman's voice in Sicily save that of its deluded King. Truth will out. By delaying the revelation of the Oracle's message, Shakespeare creates the suspense which will be sustained throughout Leontes's final confrontation with Hermione.
>
> Although we know that Apollo's words will 'clear or end the business' (line 18), the temporary illumination of optimism and faith these lines provide will be wilfully eclipsed by the King's hubris. What might have resolved in a few moments will be delayed sixteen years.
>
> Cleomenes and Dion's expressions of awe and humility contrast dramatically with Leontes's rash egotism. This scene is full of

religious **diction**: 'reverence', 'celestial', 'ceremonious', 'solemn', 'unearthly', 'rare', preparing the audience psychologically for the direct intervention into the action of Apollo in the next scene and for the priest-like role that Paulina is about to assume.

This scene functions like the play's opening scene in several ways. We overhear a conversation between two courtiers, discussing courtly business: events are reported, not witnessed. As Act I Scene 2 did not bear out the harmony presented in Scene 1, so too the events of the next scene will not bear out the hope and faith suggested here, but will be far more tragic than either Cleomenes or Dion could have imagined.

4 **celestial habits** priestly robes

17 **violent carriage** the rushed way in which it is being carried out

19 **divine** priest

20 **discover** reveal

22 **issue** outcome

SCENE 2   Hermione's trial. The Oracle's words are read out: the Queen is innocent. Leontes denounces the Oracle. Mamillius dies and Hermione faints. Immediately, Leontes repents. Paulina announces Hermione's death. Leontes resolves to visit her tomb every day

This scene consists of three closely linked episodes:

1 The court is in session. Formally, Leontes orders Hermione to be brought in and the indictment is read. She is accused of high treason, adultery and conspiracy to murder the King.

2 Hermione asserts her innocence and expresses her faith that 'powers divine' (line 27) will establish the truth. She conveys the pain, humiliation and indignity of her situation, defending the love she showed Polixenes by describing it as we saw it in Act I Scene 2, as a love, 'So and no other', which Leontes himself 'commanded' (line 65). Innocent of any conspiracy, she has no idea why Camillo left the court. Leontes tells her he has banished 'the brat' (line 86) blaming her for its fate. In looking for justice, he warns her to 'Look for no less than death' (line 90).

In her hideous situation Hermione cares little for life; Leontes's love lost, her children taken away from her, herself slandered, she can only welcome death as a relief (lines 92–107). But she will defend her honour and reputation for the sake of her children. Confidently, she appeals to Apollo's arbitration. With appropriate ceremony, the Oracle's judgement is read: 'Hermione is chaste; Polixenes blameless; Camillo a true subject; Leontes a jealous tyrant'. The baby is his own and 'the King shall live without an heir, if that which is lost be not found' (lines 131–4).

A wave of joy and relief sweeps through the court. But Leontes rashly overrules the Oracle and insists that the trial proceed. A servant rushes in with news of Mamillius's death (lines 141–3). Hermione faints. Paulina pronounces the news 'mortal': 'look down / And see what death is doing' (lines 146–7); Leontes requests that Hermione be taken and given 'Some remedies for life' (line 151).

Shocked by the death of his son, the King recognises the terrifying truth immediately: 'Apollo's angry ... / ... I have too much believed mine own suspicion' (lines 146–9). He vows to reconcile himself with Polixenes, 'New woo' (line 154) Hermione and confesses publicly his attempt to corrupt 'the good Camillo' (line 154).

3 Paulina returns to the court to announce Hermione's death. In uncompromising terms, she denounces Leontes. She accuses him of tyranny and, like a fury, recites the catalogue of his crimes of which the death of his Queen is the climax. Repentance will be in vain; he must look forward to 'nothing but despair' (line 208). Then, seeing the King 'touched / To th'noble heart' (lines 219–20) Paulina apologises for 'The rashness of a woman' (line 219) and attempts to comfort Leontes by saying that 'What's gone and what's past help / Should be past grief' (lines 220–1). Contrite, the broken-hearted King orders one grave to be made for both Hermione and Mamillius and the causes of their death to be inscribed on it to his 'shame perpetual' (line 236). He vows to visit their monument every day to the end of his life.

This climactic scene completes the tragic movement of the first half of the *The Winter's Tale*. Had Shakespeare written no more, the first three acts of this play would be his most poised, classical exercise in **tragedy**, its ending inviting comparison with the final moments of

Sophocles's *King Oedipus* (approx. 430–415BC). The regal power which Leontes has abused is finally snatched away from him when he defies not merely the processes of human justice but that heavenly authority upon which a King's mandate depends. Unlike Shakespeare's other tragic heroes, he has been in a minority of one throughout the tragic movement of the play, following his wilful blindness in defiance of the collective judgement of everyone else, on stage and in the audience. But the sustained loyalty, goodness, selflessness and foresight of others have checked Leontes from carrying out his wishes. Prevented from murdering Polixenes by Camillo, he was restrained from burning the baby by Antigonus. Having just sentenced Hermione to death, he is prevented from executing her by the divine intervention of Apollo. But for his wildest folly, his blasphemy: 'There is no truth at all i'th'Oracle' (line 138), he cannot escape scot free. Mamillius has to die to shake him sufficiently to be 'cured / Of [his] diseased opinion' (I.2.296–7).

We watch appalled and then compassionately as Leontes moves in this scene from playing the jealous tyrant to being a broken man, suddenly fully aware of the scope of the dreadful damage his wild fantasies have inflicted; appalled at what he's done, he becomes instantly rational, humble and penitent. Central to this process is the fact that it is to a woman, Paulina, the man who slandered not just his wife but the whole sex in Act I Scene 2 (lines 196–207) unconditionally submits himself.

Leontes's opening speech is characteristically pompous and arrogant. Egotistically, the King uses the regal personal pronouns 'our', 'us' and 'we' seven times in five lines (lines 1–5). When we have watched the progress of events, we hear a terrible irony in the words 'Let us be cleared / Of being tyrannous, since we so openly / Proceed in justice' (lines 4–6). The trial is merely a parade of justice; Leontes is prosecutor, judge and jury. There is no evidence against the Queen beyond his jealous fantasies. As Hermione observes, Leontes's intention to condemn her on 'surmises' and 'jealousies' is 'rigour and not law' (line 112). Ironically unaware of the anguish he will be feeling a few minutes later, he talks about his 'great grief' (line 1). Recalling Othello, absurdly he presents his jealousy as the product of having 'too much beloved' (line 4) the woman he wishes dead. But Leontes has never loved Hermione; he doesn't trust her because he appears not to know her any better than the jealous Othello knew the innocent Desdemona.

Calmly, Hermione identifies the gap between her husband's fantasy and the reality the audience has shared with her: 'My life stands in the level of your dreams' (line 80). Eloquently, yet with due deference to her husband-King, she denounces 'False accusation' and 'tyranny' (line 30) rather than Leontes himself for abusing her. Unsettled by the Queen's dignified demeanour, by her controlled, rational presentation of her case (lines 21–81), the King descends to the crude and savage language we heard him use earlier: 'You had a bastard ... / ... Thy brat hath been cast out' (lines 82–6). This is possibly the first Hermione knows of her daughter's shocking fate and that makes her death-like faint when it comes at the climax of so many hideous shocks she has suffered (line 146) utterly credible. Her powerful account of her suffering (lines 91–105) before she has recovered her strength since the birth of her daughter is increasingly concrete: 'Myself on every post / Proclaimed a strumpet' (lines 100–1) stirring feelings of pity in everyone in the theatre except Leontes.

The Oracle's judgement is brief and unequivocal. The consequences of Leontes's continued stubbornness are tragic. Retribution for his culminating act of folly and hubris is immediate and terrible. But it jolts Leontes into clear-sightedness. As hastily as he fell into his manic jealousy, immediately and unconditionally, the King's whole manner changes. He repents, acknowledging 'the heavens themselves / Do strike at my injustice' (lines 144–5). As a consequence, Paulina's torrential fury of grief (lines 174–200) serves to shift the audience's sympathies for the first time in the play towards Leontes. The imagery with which her uncompromising denunciation of the King concludes: 'naked, fasting / Upon a barren mountain, and still winter / In storm perpetual' (lines 209–11) suggests a kingdom turned into a wasteland by its ruler's folly.

Utterly humbled, whilst his lords criticise her for her 'boldness of speech', Leontes submits quietly to Paulina and to the awful truth of her just accusations. His recovery is complete, the session has, in a way he could not anticipate resulted in 'purgation' (line 7). No longer in love with jealous delusions, he insists 'Thou didst speak ... well / When most the truth' (lines 230–1). But there can be no easy relief. His daughter is lost, no one knows where, the kingdom is barren. If Leontes does not have to suffer on quite the scale Paulina envisages for a stubborn reprobate: 'A thousand knees, / Ten thousand years together' (lines 208–9), it will be sixteen years before Paulina can announce 'All my services / You have paid home' (V.3.3–4).

The scene and the first movement of the Sicilian part of *The Winter's Tale* end on a note of unqualified tragedy as movingly the broken man begs Paulina, 'Come / And lead me to these sorrows' (lines 240–1).

24 **boot me** do me any good

33 **continent** chaste, faithful

35 **Than history can pattern** than can be shown on stage

40 **prate** plead idly

43 **a derivative from me to mine** something I hand down to my children

46 **grace** favour

53–6 **I ne'er heard yet ... / ... first** Leontes is saying that people who commit evil deeds are always brazen enough to deny they have done them

75 **Wotting** if they know

85 **concerns more than avails** your denials won't do you any good

92 **commodity** pleasure

101 **strumpet** whore

104–5 **before ... limit** before I have recovered my strength after giving birth

142–3 **with mere conceit ... / ... speed** fearing what will happen to the queen

160–1 **tardied / ... command** refused to carry out my orders

174 **wheels? racks? fires?** instruments of torture

SCENE 3   Antigonus lands in Bohemia. He lays Perdita down. A
           Shepherd finds her: his son sees Antigonus savaged by a
           bear and the mariners drown

This scene consists of two linked episodes:

1 Antigonus lands on the shores of Bohemia as a terrible storm is
brewing. He recounts a dream he has had in which the spirit of
Hermione appeared to him. Weeping, she asked him to name her lost
child 'Perdita' (line 32) and informed him that as fate had chosen him
for the 'ungentle' (line 33) task of abandoning the child he would never
see his wife Paulina again. As he left Sicily before Hermione's trial,
Antigonus interprets this vision as confirmation of the Queen's guilt
and execution. He deduces it is Apollo's will the child be left in
Bohemia since she is Polixenes's daughter. He blesses Perdita, lays her
down with documents revealing her identity and a box. He turns to
make his way back to the ship but is attacked by a ferocious bear. His
final words are 'I am gone for ever' (line 157).

2 Suddenly the mood alters with the appearance of the philosophical old
Shepherd searching for his lost sheep. He discovers Perdita. His son
joins him and describes two terrible sights that he has just witnessed:
the shipwreck and drowning of all the mariners, and Antigonus being
devoured by the bear. The shepherd shows his son the child. They
open the box and discover gold. They pronounce it a 'lucky' day,
determine to keep quiet about their findings and do 'good deeds on't'
(line 133).

> thou met'st with things
> dying, I with things new-born (lines 109–10)

In this brief scene, Shakespeare manages the complex transition
from **tragedy** to **comedy**, from a mood of horrifying bleak destruction
to one full of delight, vitality and hope. Act III Scene 3 divides
almost precisely into two contrasting halves. Marking the transition
from one world of feeling to another, we move from Antigonus's
stately **blank verse** narrative to the lively **colloquial prose** of the
Shepherd. Both characters address the audience directly, it is a daring
juxtaposition of two strikingly different characters from, it seems,
two worlds of experience and feeling. But, as in Beethoven's *Pastoral*

Symphony, the experience for the audience feels like a natural progression from storm to recovery. As we watched Leontes's progress from sinner to penitent so now we witness the destructive effects of Leontes's jealousy and the gods' anger give way to the unstoppable providential progress towards new beginnings.

The action shifts from the confined and cold Sicilian court to the rugged coastline of Bohemia. In the first half of the scene the mariners and Antigonus, unaware of the Oracle's words, are carrying out Leontes's instructions. They arrive in 'ill time' (line 3). The anger of the gods at this unnatural treatment of the child is felt in the impending storm: 'the skies look grimly, / And threaten present blusters ... / The heavens with that we have in hand are angry / And frown upon's' (lines 3–6).

His compassion for Perdita ironically costs Antigonus his life. Few deaths in Shakespeare are more savage than his. The episode can be interpreted in two ways: as a bit of theatrical expediency necessary for the lubrication of the second half of the play (Perdita has to be lost for a long time), or part of the play's moral design. Antigonus and the mariners, like the innocent Mamillius, can be seen as innocent sacrificial victims swept away by the Heavens' indignation at Leontes's foul crime.

But the audience's sense of loss and tragedy is complicated immediately by the Shepherd's discordantly amusing homely preoccupations and then the relief at the discovery of the baby by someone so evidently caring, practical and principled. The Shepherd's natural and tender response to 'nurse' it (II.1.182), 'I'll take it up for pity' (line 74), contrasts dramatically with its natural father's unnatural rejection of it.

Whatever the stage effects and the audience's response to the bear have been, the Clown's disjointed, confused yet compassionate report neutralises the tragic impact of Antigonus's death and the drowning of the mariners.

The emphasis in the second half of the scene is on optimism and enthusiasm. 'Heavy matters' (line 108) are forgotten in the 'findings' (line 124), 'luck' and the mysterious bounty the Shepherd interprets as 'fairy' (line 119) gold. They serve as a passport to secure Perdita's wellbeing until she can be interesting enough for the audience to see how the pattern will be completed, the Oracle's words fulfilled.

1 **perfect** sure

1-2 **our ship ... / ... Bohemia** a crux. The real Bohemia (the present day Czech Republic) has no coastline. The scenes which follow are set firmly in the English countryside

8 **bark** ship

8-9 **I'll not ... / ... upon thee** dramatic irony. Both Antigonus and the Mariners will call out as they suffer their terrible deaths

21 **and so becoming** so graceful

22 **sanctity** holiness itself

38 **toys** silly things

40 **squared** directed

45 **Blossom** the word anticipates the way Perdita will be presented in the second half of the play as the spirit of Spring

46 **thy character** presumably a document explaining who she is

61 **wronging the ancientry** mistreating their elders

70 **some scape** illegitimate child

83 **bodkin** a little dagger

91 **hogshead** a huge barrel of beer

95 **flap-dragoned** swallowed it up

111 **bearing-cloth** christening gown

114 **changeling** a beautiful child stolen by the fairies

ACT IV

SCENE 1   Time himself appears and tells us that sixteen years have passed

Shakespeare uses the quaint device of presenting Time as an old man with wings who carries an hourglass. Acting as a **Chorus**, he tells the audience that he is going to move the action forward sixteen years. Whilst Leontes continues his repentance in Sicilia, the action which follows will take place in rural Bohemia.

The focus will fall upon Perdita and on Polixenes's son. Pointedly, Time tells us the Prince is called Florizel, a name which anticipates the **pastoral** world and the climate of regeneration we are about to enter. Perdita has grown into a wonderful young woman.

He wishes the audience an enjoyable time.

Shakespeare's play was based closely on a novel by Robert Greene called *Pandosto, or The Triumph of Time* (1588) (see Critical Approaches).

Many critics have doubted that Shakespeare wrote this speech. The mediocrity of the quaint rhyming couplets with their frequent, jarring metrical irregularities and above all the speech's diffuseness and poverty of imagery make it suspect. It recalls the perfunctory Choruses, in even poorer rhyming couplets, which open and close *Pericles* (1608), so conspicuously inferior to the magnificent **blank verse** Choruses Shakespeare wrote for *Henry V* (1599). To argue that the verse is different so that Time comes across as a distinctive, slightly ridiculous character is to ignore the fact that Shakespeare is the master of writing in many different voices: Hermione doesn't sound like Paulina and neither speaks like Florizel or the Old Shepherd. A voice can be distinctive without being inferior. It is not just the quality of the verse which is feebler than anything else in the play. The speech lacks the intensity of thought which contemplation on the processes of Time might be expected to prompt: it was a theme Shakespeare explored energetically in many of the Sonnets, for example. Here we are given little more than platitudes. The only useful information we are given is the name of Polixenes's son which the King, superfluously, gives us again in the following scene. Since Time is to triumph, he surely needs to be presented as a more interesting, authoritative and thought-provoking speaker than we have here. Failing to do a worthwhile job, the Chorus is dramatically redundant.

1 **try** test

4 **Impute it not a crime** don't object

10 **The same ... was** Time is saying that he was there before any civilisation

14 **glistering** sparkling, the word suggest, the transience of beauty

16 **my glass** Time holds an hourglass, suggesting the whole play was performed in two hours, probably a bit of **poetic licence**

22 **I mentioned a son o'th'King's** Time suggests that he is the author of the play. We heard about Polixenes's son in Act I Scene 2

24-5 **grown in grace / Equal with wond'ring** Perdita's virtuous qualities are as impressive as they are amazing, 'wonderful'

SCENE 2   Polixenes refuses Camillo's request to return to Sicilia.
           Florizel is spending his time with a shepherd's daughter.
           Polixenes determines to investigate

We see Camillo and Polixenes much aged by Time's hands. After his long stay in Bohemia, Camillo longs to return to 'lay [his] bones' (line 6) in his own country and to see and do what he can to serve Leontes, 'the penitent King' (line 6) who has urged him to return and for whom Camillo continues to care.

Polixenes pressurises Camillo to stay. He will not hear a word about 'that fatal country' (line 20) and Leontes's suffering. The memories of all that happened for Polixenes 'are even now to be afresh lamented' (line 24). He has come to depend upon Camillo so much that he will not contemplate managing his affairs without him.

Abruptly the King turns the conversation to something of more immediate concern to him: the behaviour of his son, which he regards as less than 'gracious' (line 26). Polixenes has set spies on his son and discovered that Florizel spends much of his time at the home of a remarkably wealthy shepherd who has a 'daughter of most rare note' (line 42). Polixenes orders Camillo to accompany him to the Shepherd's house where, in disguise, they will discover what his son is up to. The scene ends with Polixenes urging Camillo once again to 'lay aside … thoughts of / Sicilia' (lines 50–1). Camillo defers.

> Throughout the second half of the play, the audience is possessed of more knowledge than anyone on stage save Time himself. This means that it responds to and judges every character's words and actions with a degree of ironic detachment. With the Oracle's pronouncement, 'and the King shall live without an heir, if that which is lost be not found' (III.2.133–4) fresh in our minds, together with our knowledge of who Perdita is, the audience anticipates throughout Acts IV and V a wonderful resolution of the tragedy which was the first half of the play. Every impediment towards that resolution, therefore, strikes us as contrary to what nature, the heavens, destiny, justice, dramatic design and the human desire for happiness dictate.

> In Act IV, every detail we are given about the two kings' children makes it clear that it will be their prosperous marriage which will

complete the dramatic pattern. Until Shakespeare's final, mythical *coup de théâtre*, the excitement for the audience will be generated by the twists and turns the plot must take to reach that happy resolution.

Part of the function of Act IV Scene 2 is to keep fresh our memories of what we saw before Time's clumsy interlude – to see what seemed wholly negative as part of a larger, benevolent design. Thus it is we learn that simultaneous with Leontes's protracted suffering and repentance (and no doubt dependent upon it) has been the wonderful growth of his daughter, not dead and lost for ever, as everyone in Sicilia must assume, but thriving and, as we shall see, expressing in everything she does the spirit of regeneration, of life over death. When we hear that Polixenes's son is called 'Florizel', there can be no doubt in anyone's mind that he is this regal-rural lass's natural partner. This is why Polixenes's behaviour in Act IV Scene 2 strikes a troubling, discordant note out of all proportion to the brevity of the episode.

In fact, Shakespeare gives us more than an echo of what we saw in Leontes's behaviour at the beginning of the play. In telling Camillo how much he owes him, instead of acting generously, Polixenes sounds jealously possessive. We are reminded of another unreasonable man's refusal to let a supposedly much-loved guest have his freedom to go home. Like Leontes, Polixenes seems hurt by the idea that his guest should care for anyone but himself. Polixenes uses emotional blackmail of the most vehement, transparent kind (lines 10–20) on the man who not only saved his life but who over the last sixteen years has evidently been an invaluable courtier. Polixenes's words 'Better not to / have had thee than thus to want thee' (lines 12–13) makes him sound more like a petulant child than a grateful, magnanimous King. Like many a jealously possessive parent in Shakespeare's earlier plays, Polixenes is equally disturbed by his son's evident desire to pursue a life independent of his father.

Camillo, having encountered such regal obstinacy before, knows better than to attempt to engage in any kind of reasonable argument. Once again, he will have to fall back upon subterfuge to achieve ends even more laudable than he foresees.

1 **be no more importunate** don't press me

4 **fifteen years** a crux; this may be a printing error or a humanising touch, Camillo miscalculating how long he's been away

8 **allay** comfort

o'erween presume too much

13 **want** lack

25–8 **Kings / ... virtues** Polixenes is saying that it is as difficult for a king to cope with a son who is disobedient as with losing one who is virtuous. To compare his situation with Leontes's strikes us as extravagant

35 **eyes under my service** spies

45 **I fear, the angle** the **metaphor** recalls Leontes's feverish suspicions in Act I Scene 2 lines 180 onwards

SCENE 3   Autolycus introduces himself and robs the Shepherd's son

Like Act III Scene 3, this scene and all the others set in Bohemia take place in the open air. But where before we had a violent winter's storm, now it is Spring-cum-Summer. Shakespeare sets Act IV in a curious blend of the two seasons.

We encounter Autolycus singing exuberantly. The Clown passes on his way to buy ingredients for the sheep-shearing feast of which his sister is the mistress who 'lays it on' (line 39). Autolycus tricks the Clown by pretending to have been set upon by the notorious Autolycus. As the Clown helps him up, Autolycus filches his purse. The Clown knows all about Autolycus that 'cowardly rogue' (line 102) who 'haunts / wakes, fairs, and bear-baitings' (lines 98–9). The Clown continues on his way; Autolycus determines to go to the sheep-shearing feast to see what he can snap up there.

From the moment Autolycus strolls, singing, onto the stage, the play slips effortlessly into a higher gear. We realise with astonishment that having given us in the first half of the play a tragedy of unparalleled intensity, psychological veracity and clarity of dramatic design, Shakespeare is now going to generate a comic counterpart of unprecedented richness, colour and vitality where the dramatic impact comes not only from the beauty and variety of

Shakespeare's language but from music, dance and much ingenious stage-business and spectacle.

In Act IV Scene 3, we have a delicious taster of Autolycus's virtuosity. He enters singing of Spring. *The Winter's Tale* is undergoing a miraculous transformation, 'For the red blood reigns in the winter's pale' (line 4). His two-part song is at once a celebration of the triumph of Spring over Winter and of his delight in his roguery. Winter is past, the vitality of Spring and Summer triumphing over death: 'With heigh, the sweet birds O, how they sing!' (line 6). It is an expression of joy which recalls the opening of Chaucer's *Canterbury Tales* (1387–1400). The Clown's recital of Perdita's extravagant shopping list for the sheep-shearing feast sets the audience's sweet tooth on edge; after Winter comes a heady sensuous delight in abundance generated by the tastes, colours and smells of 'sugar, … currants, … / … saffron … warden pies; mace; … / … nutmegs, … / … ginger, … prunes, / … raisins o'th'sun' (lines 37–47).

And if Autolycus delights in his thievery, 'The white sheet … / … Doth set my pugging tooth on edge' (lines 5–7), his villainy is curiously harmless. We watch him rob the Clown but there's evidently plenty more money where that came from.

Autolycus's pretended injury 'my shoulder-blade is out' (line 72) reminds us of the naturally, perennially charitable Clown whose compassion dealt with Antigonus's remains sixteen years earlier. Although Autolycus unscrupulously takes advantage of it, the Clown's charitable nature remains uncompromised by his family's rise in fortune and will survive unchecked by whatever tricks Autolycus plays on him until the end of the play when, suddenly, their power-relationship is reversed.

2 **doxy** any 'available' woman

4 **winter's pale** pun – a) cheeks made pale by winter b) the territory that once was winter's

7 **my pugging tooth** my thieving instincts

11 **my aunts** sweethearts

14 **three-pile** best-quality velvet

19–20 **If tinkers ... / ... budget** a tinker is a tin-smith. Autolycus carries a bag made of pig-skin, so he'll look like a respectable tinker and have something to keep all the things he pinches in

23 **My traffic is sheets** Autolycus steals sheets put out on hedges to dry

26–7 **With die ... caparison** Autolycus explains that he has been reduced to wearing rags as a result of his weakness for gambling and whores

27 **my ... cheat** he makes his money by preying on gullible people

29 **the life to come** a pun – a) the future b) the after-life

31–3 **every 'leven ... / ... wool to?** the Clown is trying to work out how much money they have earned from sheep-shearing. Fifteen hundred sheep would generate a considerable income. The Shepherd and his son are very prosperous

34 **springe** trap

   cock woodcock, proverbially a particularly stupid bird

36–47 **Three pound / ... raisins o'th'sun** Perdita is preparing a tasty feast on a lavish scale

40–1 **three- / man-song men all** singers of part-songs

42 **means** counter-tenors

43 **he sings psalms to hornpipes** Shakespeare often makes fun of Puritans. This one fits sacred words even to jolly sailor's songs

44 **warden pies** pies of baked pears

85 **troll-my-dames** a gambling game where balls are rolled through holes in a board

92 **ape-bearer** a man with a performing monkey

93 **compassed a motion** took around a puppet show

98 **Prig** thief

99 **wakes** fêtes, festivals

119 **unrolled** struck off the roll of the fraternity of villains

122 **hent** grab

SCENE 4 **The sheep-shearing feast. Florizel and Perdita celebrate their love. Polixenes orders them to separate. Camillo helps them plan their elopement to Sicilia**

The scene divides into six tightly-linked episodes:
1 (lines 1–54) Perdita and Florizel, dressed for the sheep-shearing feast, declare their love for each other. But Perdita anticipates the

disapproval that their alliance must encounter when Polixenes discovers where his son's affections are 'Vilely bound up' (line 22). Florizel assures Perdita of his constancy, that if he has to make a choice, he will put her before his father. He bids her be merry and enjoy the feast as a celebration of their betrothal. Perdita hopes Fortune will smile on them.

2 (lines 55–182) The Shepherd enters with Polixenes and Camillo in disguise; he bids Perdita play her part as 'Mistress o'th'Feast' (line 68). She welcomes her guests, offering them 'flowers of winter' (line 79). Stiffly, Polixenes acknowledges these as appropriate for their ages. Perdita explains that the 'fairest flowers' (line 81) of late summer are carnations and gillyflowers, 'Nature's bastards' (line 83) which she does not care for. Although Polixenes argues cogently that 'art itself is Nature' (line 97), Perdita won't compromise. She turns to Florizel and the Shepherdesses wishing that she had 'flowers o'th'spring' (line 113) for them. Florizel conjures up a lyrical picture of her excellence (lines 135–46) and Polixenes and Camillo recognise Perdita's beauty and demeanour as 'Too noble for this place'(line 159).

The musicians strike up and the young couple join the dance of shepherds and shepherdesses. Polixenes questions the Shepherd about the 'fair swain' (line 168) who dances with his daughter.

3 (lines 183–341) A servant announces the arrival of the pedlar come to entertain them. Autolycus enters, singing his wares. He describes his ballads and Mopsa and Dorcas and he sing one of his catches together. Another servant announces the arrival of twelve herdsman who perform a satyr's dance which has been performed 'before the King' (line 335).

4 (lines 342–591) Polixenes asks Florizel why he has bought Perdita nothing from the pedlar. He replies 'She prizes not such trifles as these' (line 354), she has his heart. The Shepherd asks Polixenes and Camillo to witness the couple's betrothal. Polixenes quizzes Florizel. Has he no father? Should he not be at his son's nuptial? (line 392). Florizel insists they proceed without him. Furious, Polixenes throws off his disguise and threatens to disinherit Florizel if he sees Perdita again, condemning the Shepherd to death and Perdita to disfigurement. Immediately, he commutes these sentences but storms off, threatening dire consequences if the couple see one another again. Perdita is

downcast, but Florizel is resolute and determines to sail away from Bohemia with his shepherdess, entrusting their future to Fortune. Camillo urges caution; seeing Florizel 'irremovable' (line 504), he realises he can turn their flight to his own advantage. He proposes Florizel and Perdita make for Sicilia, and present themselves to Leontes, pretending that they come with greetings from Polixenes.

5 (lines 592–665) Autolycus returns and Camillo gives him money to swap clothes with Florizel so he and Perdita can flee in disguise. Camillo tells the audience he plans to inform Polixenes about his son's flight, hoping he'll pursue the couple to Sicilia.

6 (lines 666–836) Left alone, Autolycus reflects on his quick wit and good fortune. Loyalty to his former master persuades him to keep Florizel's flight secret. He intercepts the Shepherd and Clown who are on their way to the King. Terrified of the punishments that Polixenes may inflict on them, they intend to tell him that Perdita is not their 'flesh and blood' (line 689) and show him the fardel and the documents they found with her. Autolycus, worried that this may prevent Florizel's escape, decides he must stop the Shepherd and the Clown reaching Polixenes. Posing as a courtier, he tricks them into joining the young couple on board ship.

(The characters of Florizel, Perdita, Autolycus, the Shepherd and the Clown and their contribution to the atmosphere of this scene are discussed in some detail in Critical Approaches.)

This is the longest, richest theatrical scene Shakespeare ever created: with its songs and dances, it occupies as much stage-time as Acts II and III put together. The action is continuous in time and place.

Act IV Scene 4 paints a picture of Perdita's and Florizel's love and the focus falls almost exclusively upon them. Of the 669 lines spoken whilst they are on stage, they deliver almost half of them, more than half if we exclude the ballad-singing interlude of Autolycus and the rustics. Thereafter, Florizel speaks just thirty-five lines, Perdita only seven.

Just as in the characterisation of Autolycus, Shakespeare combines elements of **realism** and the other-worldly, so in the love-making of Florizel and Perdita, we are aware of them simultaneously as **symbolic** and as charmingly individual, lifelike characters. Our first sight of this beautiful couple is disarming. As Florizel tells us, Perdita, garlanded with flowers, looks like the spirit of Spring personified: 'no shepherdess, but Flora / Peering in April's front' (lines 2–3). We cannot but think of Leontes's wintery vigil as we register his lost daughter's robust vitality. Her festive trappings 'to each part of [her] / Does give *a life*' (lines 1–2).

Throughout the scene, we are made aware of Perdita's winning blend of healthy rustic charm and queenly grace and wit. It is not empty **hyperbole** but genuine rapture which prompts Florizel to describe the sheep-shearing as 'a meeting of the petty gods, / And [Perdita] *the queen* on't' (lines 4–5). But what we have above all in the love-making of the beautiful young couple is a spirited revision of the strange views of the two Kings in the first part of the play about the relationship between childhood innocence and mature sexuality. Perdita is frankly enthusiastic about sex as the natural, delightful expression of human love. She longs for the flowers of spring to cover Florizel: 'like a bank for Love to lie and play on, / ... quick and in mine arms' (lines 130–2). And she feels nothing grubby when she talks to Polixenes about Florizel's love as a 'Desire to breed by me' (line 103). In fact her insistence that there should be no bawdy, no 'scurrilous words' (line 215) in Autolycus's songs testifies not to her prudery but to her veneration of sex as the healthy, fruitful expression of true love. Similarly Florizel's vow of chastity before marriage 'since my desires / Run not before mine honour, nor my lusts / Burn hotter than my faith' (lines 33–5) is a sign of the strength rather than the weakness of his affection. It would be so easy for a prince to take advantage of a shepherd's daughter. Presumably that is the kind of liaison his father assumes is going on when he decides to spy on him. That what Florizel feels for Perdita is love indeed, Shakespeare develops into one of the most accomplished love poems in the language (lines 135–46). There is not space to do justice to its poetic quality in a note such as this. What makes it so evocative is a complicated patterning of key words and sounds, carefully

placed repetitions and a light rhythmic poise which makes
the whole piece read like a poem from a much later period: 'do …
Still … do … so, so … so … too … do … you … do … so … own
no … doing … So …'. It is a much more sophisticated version
of the Shepherd's animated picture of his wife (see below).

To call this scene an exercise in 'pastoral' is to confuse the furniture
for the essence. Shakespeare's rustics owe more to his experience of
the countryside in which he grew up than to the caricatures
invented by effete courtly romantic poets. They come not from
Arcadia but from Warwickshire. Even Perdita and Florizel have
come to the party from Arcadia via the robust world of *Romeo and
Juliet*.

Just as we saw the Clown 'realistically' computing his sheep-
shearing profits (Shakespeare's father had traded in wool), so we
have his father's telling Perdita to buck up her ideas with his vivid
evocation of how his old wife used to play the hostess (see Text 2 of
Textual Analysis).

By a characteristic sleight of Shakespeare's dramatic craft, we are
given the illusion that Perdita's and Florizel's love is something
we have enjoyed for some time by the delightful contrast to
such sublime affections presented by the episode of the Clown and
the two girls who are after this prosperous yokel, Dorcas and
Mopsa. 'Marry, garlic to / mend her kissing with' (lines 163–4)
captures in a single comic, sensuous detail the contrast between
the semi-divine, high-born Perdita and a country wench. The
delightful squabbling between Mopsa and Dorcas and the
chaste Clown's insistence upon 'manners' (line 242) serve as a
foil to the heady sublimity of the courtly lovers chat but also
make Perdita's graciousness plausible. And it is to this vibrant
human comedy that Autolycus contributes. After the elegant verse
of Perdita's and Florizel's romance, we get the vigorous comic prose
of the Clown and the Servant (lines 189–202). Like the Clown's
shopping list of ingredients for the feast, the inventory of the
pedlar's pack contributes to the scene's sense of vibrant abundance,
'He hath ribbons of all colours i'th'rainbow; / … inkles, caddisses,
cambrics, lawns' (lines 206–9).

In this great sheep-shearing festival, rich costume, singing and dancing generate much of the scene's splendour. It is a celebration of fertility, vitality, plenitude, joy and love: a powerful dramatic, concrete and symbolic contrast to the cold barren wastes generated by Leontes's jealousy in Sicilia. Like the pedlar, the boy actors who play the Mopsa and Dorcas are there primarily to sing and it is a twentieth-century perversity to cast these roles other than with people who can sing lustily and in tune. Similarly, for the audience, what on the page is an easily overlooked stage-direction, '*Music. A dance of Shepherds and Shepherdesses*' is in the theatre one of the highpoints of the play. This interlude effects not only a change of tone and pace which lends dramatic variety to the scene but also helps to give the Bohemian scenes the comic strength and richness which make them the counterweight to the tragic intensity of Acts I–III. Music, dancing, the high-born and the low-born lovers all whirling together in energetic fun works **iconographically** – this is vitality, this is what community looks like – directly on the feelings and indirectly on the judgement – this is human happiness.

Folk song gives way to folk dance with the eruption onto the stage of twelve satyrs. Again, the dramatic impact of this episode is easily overlooked by the reader. This fertility dance was probably a celebrated piece of 'gallimaufry' (line 326), an episode which had caused a sensation in Jonson's courtly masque *Oberon* (1611) which had indeed been 'danced before the King' (King James I). There is a sublime double-focus taking place here. The dancers are performing again both before the fictional King (Polixenes) and the real King (James): *The Winter's Tale* was given at court in February 1613 to celebrate the nuptials of Princess Elizabeth.

Much stage-time has elapsed since we first saw Perdita and Florizel. Throughout the festivities, we have watched the lovely couple together, dancing, talking. Now Shakespeare abruptly darkens 'The mirth o'th'feast' (line 42) with Polixenes's eruption of jealous possessiveness. (For a discussion of lines 388–463 see Text 3 of Textual Analysis.)

In the last part of this rich and complex scene which serves so many different dramatic functions, Shakespeare skilfully draws together all the Bohemian threads in preparation for the **denouement** and celebration of comic unity in Sicilia which will crown Act V. Somehow he must get not only Perdita, Florizel, Camillo and Polixenes across the seas, but also Autolycus, the Shepherd and the Clown if the final movement of the play is to feel like an incorporation of everything that has proved its worth, a resolution in unity of the complex chemistry which is the audience's experience of **tragicomedy**.

Because we are aware of the providential design into which everyone's destinies fit, Florizel's defiant words strike the audience as less than a 'wild dedication ... / To unpathed waters, undreamed shores' (lines 563–4) than they do Camillo. We know this apparently foolhardy pairing is absolutely right. Yet even without that knowledge, the judicious Camillo pronounces the lovers' affection 'sound' (line 376). There is thus a sublime irony when Camillo's private agenda (he will use the lovers' flight to Sicilia as a means of forcing the King to take him there) produces a pragmatic solution to the immediate problem of where the lovers will escape to and Florizel asks 'How ... / May this, almost a miracle, be done?' (lines 531–2). What Shakespeare is able to do is effortlessly endow a throw-away line with mystical resonance. It is the lightness of touch possible only when the symbolic, religious vision of 'reality' arises spontaneously from a vivid apprehension of the everyday world of affairs. Now we realise that the conversation which opened Act IV served a further dramatic function. When Camillo tells us he has 'a woman's longing' (line 663) to return to Sicilia, it is a confirmation of what we already know. This means we cannot object if whilst Paulina is stage-managing events in Sicilia, her natural partner-in-promoting-virtue, Camillo, is doing the same thing in Bohemia. As usual, Shakespeare disarms charges of theatrical expediency by having the stage manager use some theatrical jargon to accuse himself of it. Camillo tells Perdita and Florizel they must behave 'as if / The scene you play were mine' (lines 590–1) and, finding herself obliged, yet again and against her abhorrence of being 'painted' (line 101) to put on another disguise, Perdita neatly sustains the conceit, 'I see the play so lies / That I must bear a part' (lines 651–2). So much, Shakespeare seems to be saying, for the charge that the action lacks verisimilitude.

And Shakespeare's comic resourcefulness is not exhausted yet. He does more than paper over the cracks of a complicated piece of plotting. The episode between Autolycus-as-courtier, the Clown and the Shepherd is one of the funniest episodes in the whole play. The dramatic shaping is done by the shrewdly crafted variety of dramatic styles Shakespeare employs. The stratagem which exchanges Autolycus's rags for Florizel's clothes thus makes him a passable courtier for the two rustics to encounter and sets the scene for rich farce. Autolycus's latest voice, that of the affected, condescending courtier (lines 725ff) is richly satirical 'Reflect I not / on thy baseness court-contempt?' (lines 728–9), especially when we remember that this play was performed at Court. There is something Pythonesque in some of the jokes: 'We are but plain fellows, sir / A lie: you are rough and hairy' (lines 716–17); 'Advocate's the court-word for a pheasant: say / you have none' (lines 738–9); above all in the fabulous invention of tortures Autolycus promises Polixenes has in store for the Clown (lines 779–87).

Shakespeare strategically gives full rein to this knockabout humour so that the solemnity with which Act V begins can make the greatest possible dramatic contrast.

1 **weeds** clothes

2 **Flora** the goddess of flowers

3 **Peering in April's front** appearing as April begins, the spirit of Spring

6 **extremes** exaggerations

8 **mark o'th'land** person everyone talks about, looks up to

9 **swain's wearing** shepherd's outfit

10 **pranked up** dressed up in fancy clothes

10–12 **But that ... / ... accustom** if such silliness wasn't normal at a feast

22 **Vilely bound up** Perdita's **metaphor** compares Florizel to a precious book in a shabby binding

23 **flaunts** showy clothes

40 **Or I my life** dramatic irony. As events turn out Perdita's fears are well-founded, but it's as if Perdita has an intimation of the miraculous things that will be revealed

54 **red** flushed, healthy-looking

74 **rosemary and rue** evergreen, fragrant herbs associated with long-lasting friendship and repentance

79 **the year growing ancient** a crux; Shakespeare sets this scene in a season that never was. The various details offer contradictory indication of what month it is

82 **carnations and streaked gillyvors** both are cultivated plants which Perdita regards as unnatural (bastards)

93 **A gentler scion** a cutting from superior stock

95-7 **This is an art / ... art itself is Nature** Polixenes reasons that everything human beings do is part of Nature's remit; since people are naturally creative and a horticulturist is successful only if s/he understands how Nature works, there's nothing 'unnatural' in improving strains of flowers

97 **Nature** (and Nurture) Perdita's Romantic objection to 'bastardising' seems to owe something to Montaigne's essay *Of the Caniballes*, part of which is ridiculed in *The Tempest*

100 **dibble** a gardener's tool used to make holes for cuttings

101 **painted** wearing cosmetics, false-faced

116-18 **Proserpina / ... Dis's wagon** a legend retold by Ovid in *Metamorphoses* (written around 8AD): Proserpina, daughter of Ceres, the goddess of harvests, was abducted by Dis, King of the Underworld and carried away to his subterranean kingdom. After Ceres appealed to Jupiter, the King of the Gods, it was agreed that Proserpina should spend half the year above, half below the earth, which accounts for the cycle of the seasons. The allusion harmonises with Perdita's being dressed as Flora and associated throughout the play with blossom, Spring, rebirth, regeneration and hope. The passage also suggests a very well-read Shepherd's daughter

122 **Cytherea** Venus, the goddess of love

146 **all your acts are queens** we are continually reminded by her noble behaviour, and the bystanders' comments on it, that Perdita is a King's not a shepherd's daughter

149 **unstained** virtuous, honest, straight-forward

154 **turtles** turtle doves, which pair for life

171 **To have a worthy feeding** to be the owner of rich grazing land

178 **featly** elegantly

181 **that / Which he dreams not of** dramatic irony. None of the characters on stage could guess the truth which the audience possesses

190–2 **doleful ... / merrily ... very pleasant ... / ... lamentably** Shakespeare frequently makes fun of uneducated people's misprisions

195–7 **without bawdry / ... delicate burdens of dildos / and fadings, jump her and thump her** some of Autolycus's songs are full of bawdy which the innocent servant fails to detect: a dildo is an artificial penis, a fading, the sigh of orgasm. The lively rhythms of the servant's prose let us enjoy something of the 'scurrilous' songs Perdita proscribes

203 **brave** fine

204 **admirable conceited** very witty

205 **unbraided wares** fresh things to sell

207 **points** laces – the servant puns on the word as a legal term

209 **inkles** tapes

caddisses ribbons used for garters

cambrics, lawns varieties of fine linen

211 **sleevehand** cuff

212 **the work about the square** the embroidery around the yoke of the dress

221 **Cypress** fine gauze

224 **Bugle-bracelet** a bracelet of black glass beads

226 **coifs** caps

stomachers cummerbunds

228 **poking-sticks** rods used to iron starched ruffs

243 **plackets** petticoats, also slang for vaginas

245 **kiln-hole** oven door

247 **Clamor** silence

248 **tawdry-lace** silk neckerchief

250 **cozened** cheated

261 **usurer** money-lender

261–2 **brought ... / ... burden** gave birth to twenty money-bags in one go

263 **carbonadoed** scored with a knife and grilled

275 **forty thousand fathom** about fifty miles

308 **sad** serious

326 **gallimaufry** crazy mixture

346 **knacks** knickknacks

351–2 **straited / For a reply** stuck for an answer

359 **thy hand, this hand** beautiful hands were frequently objects of praise in Renaissance work, presumably because most people's hands were roughened by manual labour. How Perdita, a shepherdess has escaped calluses is a cause for wonder. Mention of her white hand reminds us of Leontes's celebration of Hermione's in Act I Scene 2

396 **altering rheums** colds in the head

405–6 **all … / … posterity** whose happiness depends upon what will happen after his death

417 **affects a sheep-hook** infatuated with a shepherdess

428 **Far than Deucalion off** as remote as the beginnings of history

462–3 **More straining … / … unwillingly** Florizel compares himself to a spirited hunting dog: the more determined the more he's held back

552 **colour** explanation, pretext

575–6 **There shall not … / … such** more dramatic irony. Camillo has no idea he is talking to Leontes's daughter

585 **furnished** dressed and provided for

606–8 **pinched a placket … / geld a … purse … / … hung** all of Autolycus's boasts have bawdy flavourings

628 **outside of thy poverty** shabby clothes

633–4 **some / boot** compensation

636–7 **half / flayed** half-skinned (undressed)

651 **undescried** unobserved (by Polixenes's spies)

696–7 **to make me / the King's brother-in-law** dramatic irony; that's exactly what he becomes in the next act

703 **fardel** little bundle

709 **excrement** beard

710 **How now, rustics!** Autolycus puts on a pompous, courtly manner

715 **discover** reveal

726 **enfoldings** clothes (he's wearing Florizel's)

727 **measure** grand way of walking, swaggering

730 **toaze** winkle out

731 **cap-à-pie** head to foot

740–1 **How blessed … / … as these are** Autolycus slips into 'courtly' blank verse

764 **handfast** under arrest

769 **germane** related

782 **aqua-vitae** strong liquor such as brandy

784 **prognostication proclaims** forecasted

819–20 **look upon the / hedge** urinate

ACT V

SCENE 1   **Leontes and three courtiers debate the question of his marrying again. Florizel and Perdita arrive. News comes that Polixenes and Camillo have landed too. Florizel begs Leontes to plead with his father on his and Perdita's behalf**

This scene takes place in the Sicilian court and consists of three linked episodes:

1 The audience sees again the wintry, childless land of Sicilia, the scene of Leontes's sixteen years of penance for his crimes. The kingdom has no heir and a debate is going on between the voices of political responsibility 'What dangers by his highness' fail of issue / May drop upon his kingdom' (lines 27–8) and Paulina's insistence that the King remain faithful to the dictates of the Oracle (lines 39–40). Leontes agrees to take another wife only at Paulina's bidding.

2 A servant announces the arrival of Florizel and his 'princess' (line 86). He is fulsome in his praise of Perdita. Paulina chides him for forgetting that Hermione 'was not to be, equalled' (line 101). The young couple appears; Leontes is struck by Florizel's likeness to his father, speechless at Perdita's beauty. He expresses his longing to see his old friend again. Florizel pretends that he has come with greetings from his father now too old to travel. He introduces Perdita as his wife, the Princess of Libya. In looking at the pair, Leontes reflects on the son and daughter that he has lost. Frankly he tells them about his sin and the heavy price he pays for it.

3 A lord rushes in with greetings from Polixenes and a plea to seize Florizel and the Shepherdess he has run off with. Hurrying to the court, Polixenes and Camillo have encountered the Shepherd and his son. Florizel is dismayed that Camillo has betrayed him, Perdita fears for her 'father' (line 201). Florizel confesses that he and Perdita are not yet married and begs Leontes to plead his case to Polixenes. Readily, the King agrees.

It's difficult to imagine a greater dramatic contrast to the colour, music and vitality of the sheep-shearing scene, than the return to the barren Sicilian court. Here nothing has changed, there has been no growth. All we see are people we've seen before, now sixteen years older, more wrinkled, greyer. Leontes has become the man dwelling 'by a churchyard' of Mamillius's Winter's Tale (II.1.30). We hear just enough (lines 6–69) to tell us that the broken King's grief and sense of sin are as intense as they were when we left him at the end of Act III Scene 2.

The common-sense pragmatism of Cleomenes and Dion is countered by the sharp, uncompromising tones of Paulina. What are being tested and demonstrated to the audience are the King's humility and constancy. We are left in no doubt of his sincerity, expressed by his unequivocal submission to Paulina's insistence that he may marry only 'when [his] first queen's again in breath / Never till then'(lines 83–4). Whereas Paulina's intransigence might strike a first-time audience as insensitive, the arguments of Cleomenes and Dion strike an audience who knows the play as short-sighted and potentially mischievous: if Leontes followed their advice, he'd commit bigamy. In both cases, what is being illustrated is how we make mistakes when we are unable to see the complete picture.

The language of the first eighty-three lines is highly charged. All four speakers use religious vocabulary: 'saint-like', 'redeemed', 'penitence', 'trespass', 'Heavens', 'evil', 'virtues', 'holy', 'holier', 'bless', 'the gods', 'divine', 'Oracle', 'sainted spirit', 'tempt'. And Paulina, playing a sublime game as Leontes's confessor, weaves into this opening section an intimation of something 'monstrous to our human reason' (line 41). This lofty game is being played not only with Leontes but with the audience too.

The play will conclude with a miracle. When it happens, it works because we have been so carefully, but subliminally, prepared for it. Paulina thinks it is as unlikely that Perdita will be found as that her husband Antigonus should 'break his grave / And come again to me' (lines 42–3). People do not return from the dead and Shakespeare took a lot of trouble to show us Antigonus destroyed by the bear. Yet the audience knows that Perdita is about to arrive.

We realise that what's 'monstrous to our human reason' can happen.

So the other impossibility which Leontes and Paulina's conversion (lines 49–84) weaves around, sounds sometimes like the profound tragic regret of what might have been: 'I might have looked upon my queen's full eyes, / Have taken treasure from her lips' (lines 53–4), sometimes like a riddle 'No more such wives, therefore no wife' (line 56). Sometimes it sounds like a nightmare: 'would make her sainted spirit / Again possess her corpse' (lines 57–8), sometimes like a grim joke: 'Were I the ghost that walk'd ... / ... I'd shriek, that even your ears / Should rift' (lines 63–6), sometimes like a lovely fantasy: 'Unless another, / As like Hermione as is her picture, / ... such / As walked your first queen's ghost, it should take joy / To see her in your arms' (lines 73–81), only finally as a frank impossibility: 'when your first queen's again in breath' (line 83). In the excitement of Perdita's arrival and the reconciliation with Polixenes which ensues, our conscious minds forget these pregnant fragments. But through them Shakespeare has erected the psychological scaffolding for his theatrical master-stroke.

What for the court is the wholly unexpected arrival of the lovely young couple in the static, grief-bound Sicilia where Leontes has been trapped in the past brings a sudden startling injection of youthful beauty, healthy energy and the prospect of new life. Suddenly things are moving precipitously again, but this time out of the depths towards a wonderful resolution. When Leontes tells the heirs to both kingdoms they are as welcome 'As is the spring to th'earth' (line 151) we feel the rich irony of the play's title, register afresh the force of Perdita's self-identification with Proserpina in Act IV Scene 4. These phrases are more than **metaphorical** colouring. The language is an explicit celebration of the end of the tragic process. Florizel and Perdita's arrival really does 'Purge all infection from our air' (line 168).

28–9 **devour / Incertain lookers-on** cause people disastrous anxiety

29–30 **What ... / ... is well** the first of many examples of the complex **dramatic irony** by which the audience is subliminally prepared for the miracle with which the play ends

35 **Respecting** compared with

41 **as monstrous to our human reason** beyond anything common sense could imagine

46 **issue** a) heir b) the consequences

53–4 **I might have looked ... / ... from her lips** more dramatic irony. Shakespeare anticipates meticulously the action of the final scene

57–8 **her sainted spirit / ... stage** more of the same

66 **rift** split

90 **out of circumstance** without the ceremony befitting a royal visit

92 **train** attendants

94 **peerless piece of earth** God's masterpiece (human beings having been created by God from clay)

105–6 **when she has ... / ... tongue too** when you have seen her, you will praise her too

108 **professors else** members of all other religions and sects

     proselytes disciples

122 **Unfurnish me of reason** in Act V, Leontes's leaving the world of 'common sense' is as positive as it was negative in Act I

123 **Your mother was most ... wedlock** a curious reminder of the misogynous Leontes of Act I

126 **hit** precisely caught

130 **princess-goddess** the startled movement of the words catches Leontes's astonishment

139 **at friend** in the way of friendship

149–50 **interpreters / ... slackness** remind me how I've neglected my duties towards him

155 **adventure of her person** risking her life

164 **bend** continue their journey

181 **attach** arrest

206 **the odds for high and low's alike** Fortune treats people the same, irrespective of their social rank

222 **I'd beg your precious mistress** Paulina hears Leontes's words as dangerous. In Robert Greene's *Pandosto* (1588) the King finally kills himself for having been incestuously attracted to his own daughter

229 **Your honour not o'erthrown by your desires** providing you have not yet made love

SCENE 2 We hear how Camillo and Leontes are reunited, the Oracle's predictions fulfilled, and the two Kings reconciled

This scene consists of three linked episodes:

1 Autolycus begs for information and we learn what has happened by report from three courtiers. The bundle which was with Perdita when the Shepherd discovered her has been opened and her identity revealed. The passionate reunions between Leontes and Camillo and then Polixenes are described. We hear about Paulina's grief as she heard about her husband's savage death, her joy at Perdita's safe recovery. Leontes has moved all hearers with his frank confession of how Hermione died. We learn that the royal company is now visiting Paulina's house where Julio Romano has executed a statue of Hermione which is amazingly lifelike.

2 Excluded from the celebrations, Autolycus, crestfallen, explains how his scheme to explain everything aboard ship to Prince Florizel was frustrated by the weather which made the royal couple sea-sick.

3 He is joined by the Shepherd and Clown who enter in their smart new gentlemen's clothes. Their comic narrative develops what we have heard already. Now acknowledged members of the royal family, we see that their natures are unchanged. Autolycus begs their forgiveness and asks the Shepherd's son to give a good report of him to Prince Florizel. The Clown agrees so long as Autolycus mends his ways. The rogue promises to do his best and all three leave to join the others for the final scene.

This scene comes as a shock to the audience. After the excitement built up in Act V Scene 1, we anticipated the play ending in a comic resolution of tensions, Leontes miraculously being reunited with his lost child, the furious Polixenes discovering with delight that his son has chosen, by intuition, a princess for his bride, the two old friends reconciled, Paulina's, Camillo's and the Old Shepherd's services appropriately rewarded, the two kingdoms united in a greater prosperity than could ever have been anticipated, poetic justice triumphant. The shock comes not from the absence of these ingredients but from Shakespeare's method of presenting them. No matter how rich the language, narrated events cannot have the impact of a direct theatrical presentation: there is something missing, we feel disappointed by this 'broken delivery' (line 9) by minor characters. Surely this isn't the dramatic climax we have been waiting for?

It's not as if the dramatic climax is not simply delayed by these 170 lines of **prose**. Until the end of this scene, it looks as if there won't be one, as if the play will fizzle out, using the convention of a Greek **Chorus** to describe things which cannot be shown adequately on stage. This is the only time Shakespeare plays such a trick on his audience. It is at once the most daring and the most powerful piece of theatre he ever engineered.

But the prose is not as undistinguished or as simply functional as it may seem. First we have the poignancy of Autolycus, hitherto the rogue in control, now pointedly, pathetically, on the periphery of events, begging for news.

Then there is the extravagant language of the courtiers. It recalls the prose of the opening scene. But whereas there we felt an unwarranted straining for effect, an attempt to elaborate something which turned out to be hollow, here the language is stretched in an attempt to express the all but inexpressible: 'amazedness', 'admiration', 'wonder', 'extremity', 'Such a deal of wonder' (lines 5–24). What has happened not only outstrips the resources of 'ballad-makers' (line 25) such as Autolycus who, we remember 'carry lies abroad' which they pretend to be wonders (IV.4.269) but tax the expressive capabilities of the most accomplished speakers. We are dealing with things 'to be seen [which] cannot be spoken of' (line 42). Some people might be reminded of the twentieth-century philosopher Wittgenstein.

In any other context to talk of 'a world destroyed, or one ransomed' (line 15) would be **hyperbole** and the description of Leontes 'being ready to leap out of himself' (line 48) ridiculous. But we are in a world of extraordinary, miraculous but keenly felt experiences here. The Shepherd is at once the kindly old man who nurtured Perdita and 'like a weather-bitten conduit of many kings' reigns' (line 54). In the lightest possible way, Shakespeare is evoking a sense of the transcendent in the concretely particular place and time. The phrase, 'Like an old tale still' (line 59) is more than a rhetorical trick to suspend our disbelief. It develops the feeling that has been growing throughout the play that this drama is at one level a tale older than recorded history. That like folk tales, myths and legends, it is 'true' in a sense which makes 'human reason' (V.1.41) look pretty limited. It is the latest and most dramatic expression of a recognition which dawns upon many characters towards the end of Shakespeare's greatest plays. We are reminded of Hamlet's, 'There's a divinity which shapes our ends, rough-hew them how we will' (*Hamlet*, V.2.9–10).

At the point where opposites and paradoxes cluster most thickly together, 'lost', 'found', 'noble combat', 'joy and sorrow', 'declined', 'loss', 'elevated', 'fulfilled' (lines 70–3) comes the merest hint of what's still to come. Perdita's grief for her mother was so intensely moving that 'Who was most marble there changed colour' (line 88). Four lines later we hear first of Hermione's 'statue' – 'he so near to Hermione hath done Hermione that they say one would speak to her and stand in hope of answer' (lines 97–100). The ingredients for the spectacular are all prepared.

Shakespeare, though, makes one concession to those whose faith is weaker than their need for a 'naturalistic' explanation of what is coming. The lame lines of the Second Gentleman 'I thought ... / ... that removed house' (lines 102–5) are a clumsy concession to the sceptics. They raise more questions than they answer. What Hermione and Paulina have 'really' been up to, cannot withstand any kind of psychologising.

After the high-flown **prose** style of the first part of the scene, the audience needs a marked change of pace and tone if it is not to suffer ecstasy exhaustion before the final coup. What we get is not 'comic relief' but 'comic intensification', a different perspective on the mysterious workings of grace, in different, more earthy voices. It is an effect the writers of *The Towneley (or Wakefield) Second Shepherds' Play of the Nativity* (fourteenth century) employed.

From line 111 onwards, we move from a courtly register 'Every wink of an eye some new grace / will be born' (lines 108–9) to the familiar homely **rhythms** and **diction** of Autolycus. Yet even his language is charged with mystical overtones. He has no 'benefit of access' (line 108) to the world where 'Every wink of the an eye some new grace is born'. His pranks prevent 'preferment drop[ping] on [his] head' (line 112) whilst the Shepherd and his son are 'already appearing in the blossoms of their fortune' (line 123). Shakespeare carefully balances our sense of Providential and earthly mechanisms at work here. By the end of the scene the same natural practical charity which distinguished the Shepherd and his son when we first met them in Act III Scene 2, will rescue Autolycus from his lonely position on the outskirts of things. In spite of his 'former life' (line 111) and his 'other discredits' (line 120), he too, like Leontes, will be given another chance.

The phrase 'gentleman born' is repeated seven times in just ten lines (lines 125–35) and 'gentleman-like', 'gentle', 'gentlemen' and 'gentleman' (twice) all crop up in the next twenty. Shakespeare forces us to dwell on the words and so ask the question what does 'gentle' mean, after all? Perhaps he was thinking of Chaucer's *Ballade of Gentilesse* (*c*.1390) and its insistence that true gentility has nothing to do with rank, everything to do with decency, practical virtue. By a clever movement we see that Honesty and Trust, in the shape of the Clown, are not as foolish as Autolycus imagined (IV.4.592). The young man sees the rogue for what he is: 'I know thou art no tall fellow / of they hands, and that thou wilt be drunk' (lines 161–2). But his generosity is stronger than his disappointment. And so, unlike the case of Malvolio at the end of *Twelfth Night* (1600), the final resolution will include even the man who has done everything in his limited power to keep off the path of virtue. It is a reflection of the two Kings' magnanimity, 'the two kings called my father brother' (lines 137–8): such a marked relief from the endings of Shakespeare's earlier **comedies** where at the end the courtiers unite to scoff at the rustics.

2 **relation** narration
31 **pregnant by circumstance** proved by evidence

35 **character** handwriting

52 **clipping** embracing

55–6 **lames / ... to do it** it's beyond the wit of man to describe it faithfully

60 **though credit be asleep** even if people find it impossible to believe

62 **innocence** a) simplicity b) honesty

86 **dolour** grief

95 **Julio Romano** a pupil of Raphael, the only contemporary artist Shakespeare ever mentions

97 **beguile Nature of her custom** steal Nature's customers away from her

109–10 **unthrifty to our / knowledge** missing the opportunity to learn more

112 **preferment** rewards, promotion

143 **preposterous estate** a malapropism; what the Clown intends to say is 'prosperous estate'

155–6 **boors / and franklins** peasants and yeomen (i.e. people who are now further down the social ladder than he is)

160 **tall fellow of thy hands** a brave chap

SCENE 3 **The royal party is at Paulina's house. They visit the chapel where Hermione's statue is unveiled. It comes to life. The pattern is complete**

Leontes thanks Paulina formally for her sixteen years of 'comfort' (line 1), equally formal, liturgical-sounding is her response: 'All my services / You have paid home' (lines 3–4). The shriven Leontes, Polixenes and their children, with Camillo and other courtiers have been admiring the works of art in the gallery in Paulina's house. Now they enter the chapel and we await the climax: the unveiling of Hermione's statue. When Paulina draws the curtain, there is a stunned silence. The statue is extraordinarily lifelike but this is *not* the Hermione we saw earlier. As both Kings remark, it is the statue of a much older woman. Paulina explains that the skilful sculptor has presented Hermione as she would be now. Leontes recognises in the figure the 'majesty' of the woman he first wooed. Perdita kneels and asks the statue's blessing.

Leontes is so moved that Paulina offers to close the curtain lest the sight of the statue prove unbearable. Leontes thinks he even senses breath from the figure and is about to kiss the statue when Paulina tells them all they must either leave the chapel immediately or 'awake [their] faith' (line 95). Music plays and, prompted by Paulina, miraculously, Hermione's statue comes to life. Leontes and his Queen, apparently risen from the dead, embrace. Paulina presents the Queen's lost daughter to her and finally Hermione speaks. Leontes unites Paulina and Camillo in marriage and the whole company, 'precious winners all' (line 131), is led by Paulina out of the chapel.

> The technique of it is mature, that of a man who knows he can do what he will, lets himself in for difficulties with apparent carelessness, and overcomes them at his ease. (Harley Granville-Barker, *Preface to The Winter's Tale*, 1912)

This scene raises many questions for those on stage and for the audience, but to ask them is to miss the point entirely. It is not a scene to respond to with the head, but with the heart and that is the 'wonder' (line 22) of it. Blasphemy laws in Shakespeare's time were strict and miracles smack of Popery. In this scene, Paulina's role comes as close to that of a priest, the action to that of a religious ceremony as is compatible with presentation on a commercial stage. Her words, 'It is required / You do awake your faith' (lines 94–5), which recall those of the Communion service, is an instruction to actors and audience alike. '*If* you can behold it,' says Paulina to Leontes 'I'll make the statue move'(lines 86–7). This wholly unexpected but utterly fitting climax to the play (there is no parallel in Robert Greene's *Pandosto* – 1588) is about what we are prepared and ready to see and believe. What happens is incredible; it's 'magic' (line 110). For sixteen years Leontes thought he had seen Hermione 'dead' (line 140); that she is living 'should be hooted at / Like an old tale' (lines 16–17). All the characters express their sense of 'marvel', disbelief and 'amazement' (lines 100, 87).

The dramatic impact of this scene lies in the length of time that Hermione stands motionless. We must register her as 'dead' to feel that electric frisson which regularly ripples through the theatre as death is conquered. The actress playing the role, must rise to an 'impossible' challenge: appear absolutely still for eighty lines whilst everyone gazes at her.

Yet reports of performances over the last hundred years or so, consistently attest to the fact that actresses pull it off, that the trick

is overwhelmingly successful. And this thrill of delight for the
audience does not diminish but increases the more familiar it is
with the play. That is why the scene works more like religious ritual
than conventional drama. No matter how many times somebody
takes Communion, the words 'Draw near with faith' (from *The
Book of Common Prayer*, 1559) are the prelude to a mystery. This is
not to argue that Shakespeare's play is some kind of Christian
allegory. It is insistently larger than that. But the kind of experience
he is exploring here is religious, archetypal, not simply theatrical.

What is so emotionally moving and satisfying about this episode is
the feeling that, wonderfully, the 'heavens directing' (line 150) there
can be second chances, that people can be forgiven for their
mistakes. Simply that what's 'lost' can be 'found'.

Yet Shakespeare doesn't abandon psychological **realism** here. It is
poignant that at this moment when Leontes does, in effect 'new-
woo' (III.2.156) his wife, there are no words at all. Words failed in
Act I Scene 2 and here there is too much to be said, by both of them
and no possibility at such a juncture of verbalising anything. If any
moment in this play needs to be seen in the theatre rather than read,
it is this reunion. All Shakespeare gives us are the stage directions
Polixenes and Camillo provide: 'She embraces him. / She hangs
about his neck' (lines 111–12). It is a masterstroke to give Camillo
an image which recalls Leontes's words at his most deluded: 'Why,
he that wears her like a medal, hanging / About his neck, Bohemia'
(I.2.307). Now Leontes knows she is his, and can feel it.

(Paulina's role in this scene is discussed more fully in
Characterisation.)

12 **singularities** rarities
56 **Will piece up in himself** add to his own (grief)
58 **wrought you** made you suffer excessively
77 **cordial** restorative
101 **I'll fill your grave up** since you are alive you have no need for a grave
113 **If she pertain to life** if she lives

PART THREE

CRITICAL APPROACHES

CHARACTERISATION

Characterisation is the art of giving each person in a story not only distinctive attitudes, values and behaviour but also a distinctive voice. It is his ability to present with unusual vitality and detachment so many different sorts of characters and to give each of them their own ways of expressing themselves which raises Shakespeare above most other writers. In discussing his characters, therefore, it is important to look at both *what* they say and *how* they say it.

LEONTES

Leontes's character is discussed both in the Summaries and Commentaries and in Text 1 of the Textual Analyses.

POLIXENES

Polixenes's character is also discussed both in the Summaries and Commentaries (especially Act IV Scene 2) and in Text 3 of the Textual Analyses.

MAMILLIUS

Mamillius's character is considered in Text 1 of the Textual Analyses and in the Theme on Children and Childhood.

HERMIONE

Hermione is a 'good' (I.2.220) and 'gracious' (I.2.233) queen; a 'rare' and 'precious creature' (I.2.452) 'unparalleled' (V.1.16) in beauty and honour and 'spotless / I'th'eyes of heaven' (II.1.131–2). When we see her first she is poised, relaxed and witty, playing the gracious hostess as her husband commands her to do. She is a loving and generous wife and mother, an obedient and loyal queen.

Once she is wrongfully accused, she shows extraordinary dignity, courage, humility, patience and faith. Despite the injustice to herself and the loss of both her children, she never once blames or accuses Leontes, but shows rather a concern for the unhappiness which he will inevitably bring upon himself (II.1.96–8). She is able to manage her suffering by weaving it into a larger pattern 'I must be patient till the Heavens look / With an aspect more favourable' (II.1.106–7). Yet although she copes with her suffering by regarding it as some kind of Providential trial, Hermione is no meek and mild Desdemona (the main female character in *Othello*). For example, in the trial scene (Act III Scene 2), until she faints at the news of her son's death, Shakespeare gives her three times as many lines as her tyrannical husband and powerfully contrasts his wild verbal barbarisms with Hermione's quiet, forceful eloquence. Where Paulina's is strident, Hermione's language is beautifully controlled, strong in its gentle **diction** and irrefutable logic. She does not need to play the virago: she sounds like a totally secure adult dealing with a violently deluded but much loved child. High-born, majestic, but never pompous, 'The Emperor of Russia … / … not revenge' (III.2.118–22), hers is the eloquent stoicism we associate with the heroines of Greek tragedy.

PERDITA

Shakespeare's skill in characterisation is nowhere more masterly than in his realisation of Perdita. He has set himself a formidable task. She must be at once credible as her mother's daughter, the Shepherd's foster-child, the Clown's sister, Florizel's natural partner, the spirit of regeneration personified and an engaging individual.

Shakespeare skilfully weaves many different types of poetry together to generate this composite picture. If it is Hermione's daughter who affirms 'affliction may subdue the cheek, / But not take in the mind' (IV.4.573–4) it's Mopsa's friend who mocks Camillo's courtly praise, 'Out, alas! / You'd be so lean that blasts of January / Would blow you through and through.' (IV.4.110–12). When, in Act V Scene 2, the gentleman confirms the impression we have already been given: 'the majesty of the creature in resemblance / of the mother' (lines 35–6) he is speaking of both Perdita's looks and the way she talks. There is a strong case for having the role played by the actress who played Hermione in the first half of the play. After sixteen years, Hermione is likely to look less like she did in Act III than her daughter is. Since Hermione and Perdita appear together only in the final scene, it is possible to juggle things so that a single actress effectively plays both parts: as Judi Dench did in the celebrated RSC production in 1969.

Despite his prejudices, Polixenes cannot help but feel 'nothing she does or seems / But smacks of something greater than herself, / Too noble for this place' (IV.4.157–9) whilst Camillo judges her simply 'The queen of curds and cream' (IV.4.161). Shakespeare combines in Perdita a diversity of qualities. Nothing in Shakespearean verse paints a more engaging picture of a lovely girl than Florizel's poem (IV.4.135–46) combining as it does a delighted sense of her vivacity, poise and grace in everything she does. She is as accomplished in buying and selling as in dancing, in singing as in ordering her household affairs. At once ardent and chaste, she is witty, strong-willed and modest.

As well as the beauty and dignity which she has inherited from her mother, she also shares Hermione's humility and strength of character. When things go wrong, she accepts her fate: her 'dream' shattered, she'll 'queen it no inch farther' (IV.4.445–6). And like Hermione for Leontes, her concern is more for Florizel than for herself. But although accepting, she shows an inner faith and is disgusted by Polixenes's arrogance: 'I was about to speak and tell him plainly, / The selfsame sun that shines upon his court / Hides not his visage from our cottage, but / Looks on alike' (IV.4.440–3).

Perdita's recovery marks the shift from winter to spring and purges Leontes's court of past sins. It heralds the beginning of a new life for her mother, her father and the kingdom.

FLORIZEL

In a sonnet dedicated to Florio (1591 – see Peter Levi, The Life and Times of William Shakespeare, Macmillan, 1988), Shakespeare plays on the name's associations:

> Sweet friend, whose name agrees with thy increase,
> How fit a rival art thou of the spring!

The Kings' children, their stake in the future, Florizel and Perdita are natural partners, together the embodiment of the spirit of renewal. Just as

Perdita physically resembles her mother, so Florizel bears a striking resemblance to his father (V.1.123–7). Polixenes waxes lyrical about his son in Act I Scene 2 but we do not learn about either his significant name until Time reveals it in Act IV Scene 1, or his character until we meet him Act IV Scene 4 when he has grown into a young man in the process of rebelling against his father.

Florizel's youth and faith provide the necessary contrast to the age and bitterness of Leontes and Polixenes. From the beginning of Act IV Scene 4 we see Florizel as the single-minded servant of love. In equal measures ardent and respectful, he sees his chance encounter with Perdita 'When my good falcon made her flight across thy father's ground' (lines 15–16) as providential. To every expression of Perdita's common-sense anxieties about what will ensue when, inevitably, his father opposes their union, Florizel's energetic responses are unequivocal 'Or I'll be thine … Or not my father's. For I cannot be / Mine own … if / I be not thine. To this I am most constant, / Though destiny say no' (IV.4.42–6) – a resolution the progress of the scene confirms. It is his faith and constancy which survive the test and carry Perdita back to Sicily, see the Oracle fulfilled and lead to the final reconciliation and unification of the two kingdoms.

CAMILLO

The symbolic role of Camillo is discussed in the section on Imagery.

Like Paulina, Camillo is both a fully realised, engaging character and an important cog in the dramatic mechanism.

One of the touchstones of decency and sanity against which the audience can measure the behaviour of other characters in the play, Camillo is the latest in a long line of selfless, fiercely loyal servants to Shakespearean kings. His 'worth and honesty / Is richly noted' (V.3.144–5) by Leontes, Hermione, Polixenes and Florizel; his judgements of them help shape the way the audience regards their behaviour.

It is clear from the opening scene that he knows Leontes intimately. Promoted by him 'from meaner form / … benched and reared to worship' (I.2.313–14), he has risen by merit, (I.1.391–4) to become a man of standing, substance and reputation in the Sicilian court who carries 'great

authority' (II.1.53). He has long been his master's confidante and
counsellor, 'I have trusted thee, Camillo, / With all the nearest things to
my heart ... / My chamber-counsels' (I.2.235–7). It is natural, therefore,
that Camillo is the first to hear of Leontes's jealous fantasies and, since
he is equally loyal to the Queen and to the truth, equally natural that,
boldly, he should challenge Leontes's misreading of Hermione's
behaviour. By refusing to carry out Leontes's instructions to poison
Polixenes, Camillo risks his own life to prevent the King becoming a
murderer.

During the sixteen years he serves Polixenes, this King, too, comes
to respect Camillo 'as a father'(I.2.461). At the end of Act IV Scene 4,
forced again to betray one master in order to help another, Camillo's
stage-managing role harmonises with Paulina's and makes their marriage
at the end of the play fitting in both practical and human terms.

PAULINA

As with Camillo, Paulina's symbolic role is discussed in the section on
Imagery.

Paulina was the name of the wife of the Roman stoic philosopher
Seneca. Their physical courage, philosophical strength and devoted
love for one another is described in Montaigne's essay, *Of Three Good
Women* which Shakespeare's friend Jean Florio translated into English
(1595).

The Winter's Tale is remarkable for presenting three women as the
strongest characters in the play. Paulina is the most earthy of these: her
tongue with its biting **colloquialisms** is naturally 'audacious' (II.3.42). As
Antigonus's wife, a woman of standing, she not only outfaces the timid
male courtiers who surround Leontes, 'Let him that makes but trifles of
his eyes / First hand me' (II.3.62–3) but motivated by nothing but an
ardent refusal to compromise with 'weak-hinged fancy' (II.3.118), frankly
tells the King he is 'mad' (II.3.71).

Happy to be seen as a descendent of Chaucer's Dame Partlet the
Hen (II.3.75) fearless, bustling, eloquent and witty, she plays the scourge,
verbally lashing Leontes first for his 'dangerous, unsafe lunes' (II.2.30)
then for 'killing' his Queen (III.2.173ff). But she's quick to recognise
when she has wounded a genuinely grieving man 'Alas, I have showed

too much / The rashness of a woman' (III.2.218–9) and assumes thereafter the counselling role previously performed by Camillo. From the moment of Leontes's submission to her (III.2.212) she is presiding moral authority in the Sicilian court. It is she who leads Leontes to his penitential sorrows at the end of the first half of the play, she who conducts the whole company of 'precious winners all' (V.3.131) off stage at the end of the second.

Paulina's passionate and volatile words are motivated by nothing but selfless duty. She shows patience managing her private grief for her husband's death for which she never reproaches the King.

Autolycus

Autolycus is one of Shakespeare's most original and vibrant creations. His name, which comes from Homer, suggests a predatory wolf but his own description of himself as 'a snapper up of unconsidered trifles' (IV.3.25–6) with 'a merry heart' (IV.3.123) is more in character with the engaging rascal Shakespeare presents. A natural performer, who at one time had his own puppet show, 'a motion of the Prodigal Son' (IV.3.93–4) he is now a travelling salesman; most of his goods are counterfeit and his boast that 'They throng who should buy first, as if my trinkets had been hallowed and brought a benediction to the buyer' marks him out as a direct descendant of Chaucer's Pardoner (see *The Canterbury Tales*, *c*.1400), a fake medicine man. Where Paulina and Camillo perform what strike others as miracles, Autolycus hawks ballads describing false wonders (IV.4.260–82).

Autolycus is an ambiguous character. He is at once robustly realistic, a character drawn from London low-life, the perennial haunter of 'wakes, fairs, and bear baitings' (IV.3.99) whose 'revenue is the silly cheat' (IV.3.27) and at the same time a mythical type: the timeless rogue who, despite his cunning, is used by Providence to promote rich ends. As the Shepherd sees, 'He was provided to do us good.' (IV.4.830)

He is a wonderful singer. The Servant's enthusiastic advertisement 'He sings / several tunes faster than you'll tell money' (IV.4.185–6) makes the simple point that if Autolycus is a con man, he is also an artist, a comic genius, a maker of mirth, a source of energy, 'He hath songs for man or woman, of all sizes' (IV.4.193).

If he steals people's money, Autolycus gives them something worth more than money. Like Falstaff, he generates, radiates fun whenever he is on stage; any damage he does is more theoretical than something experienced. And like Falstaff, he is 'not only witty in himself but the cause of wit in other people' (*2 Henry IV*, I.2.11).

Not only is Autolycus a fine singer, he is an accomplished actor, master of many voices. He swindles the Clown three times but each Autolycus (the footpad's victim, the pedlar and the courtier) is a fresh incarnation. The role calls for a charismatic actor.

Autolycus holds centre stage and enjoys a privileged relationship with the audience. He confides in us and throughout the action of Acts IV and V shares with us his problems and his disappointments. Where Leontes's mad confessions alienate the audience, Autolycus's disclosures are engaging; they charm away any inclination to censure him. We are half-aware that he is not as completely his own master as he believes, 'For the life to come, I / sleep out the thought of it' (IV.3.29–30) but when the Clown's and the Shepherd's charity incorporates him into the joyful celebrations from which his roguery properly exclude him (V.2.169) it feels a just recognition of the positive spirit, the inventive, comic energy he has breathed into the play. In spite of himself, he is effectively enrolled in 'the book / of virtue', a prospect which seemed simply ridiculous (IV.3.119–20).

Shakespeare gives Autolycus an important **soliloquy** 'what a fool Honesty is' (IV.4.592), a theme which has preoccupied Shakespeare throughout his career: *King Lear* (1605) is simply the most sustained and searching exploration of the idea. Reminiscent once again of Chaucer's Pardoner, Autolycus boasts of his swindling 'I have sold / all my trumpery … / … as if my / trinkets had been hallowed and brought a benediction to / the buyer' (IV.4.593–9).

What is Shakespeare to do with this cut-purse, liar, self-seeking parasite? Is he to be excluded from the final picture, clumsily woven into it or incorporated? One of the first things Autolycus told us about himself was that once he had been Prince Florizel's man. What emerges in the closing section of Act IV is that in spite of his honest roguery, Autolycus has an affection for the young man which works directly against his own self-interest. It is an oddly humanising touch.

THE SHEPHERD AND THE CLOWN

If they are unlettered, the Shepherd and his son are recognised by the audience to be thoroughly decent, respectable characters long before their elevation to the rank of 'gentlemen' in Act V Scene 3. If the Shepherd's charity is of a practical kind 'bid / These unknown friends to's welcome, for it is / A way to make us better friends, more known' (IV.4.64–6) it is of a piece with the spontaneous kindness which took up the child and left his valuable sheep in Act III Scene 2.

The Clown 'who has not only his / innocence, which seems much, to justify him' (V.2.62–3) is much more than simply Autolycus's dupe. Shakespeare very carefully balances his gullibility, his delicious verbal absurdities with his radiant good nature and evident prosperity. And when it comes to the point in Act V Scene 2 we see that Autolycus has not so completely hoodwinked the young man as he thinks!

THEMES

When you know the text well, studying a work of literature encourages you to stand back from the action and think about some of the ideas and issues the story explores. Critics call such ideas and issues 'themes'. Like musical themes in a symphony or an opera, they weave in and out of the whole work, hold it together and establish its particular tone and atmosphere. Often examiners ask candidates to discuss the way a particular theme is explored in a play. It is a way of allowing you to show you are aware of the connections between lots of different details in the play. To do this task well, you must know the text thoroughly, and use lots of brief, appropriate quotations to develop the argument beyond vague generalisation.

The Winter's Tale explores many themes, such as what the relationship should be between Nature and Art; the interconnection between human time and the progress of the seasons; how the old must give way to the new; the nature of jealousy and of true love; masculine and feminine versions of 'strength', and the contrast between the world of the court and the world of the countryside. You will find these themes explored in the commentaries and textual analyses. In a guide as brief as this one, we can suggest only a handful of other themes you may wish to think about as your grasp of the play becomes ever more secure.

A PPEARANCE AND REALITY, FORTUNE AND PROVIDENCE

Some themes interested Shakespeare throughout his creative life and run through many of the plays and poems.

For example, working in the theatre prompted Shakespeare to think about how the real world was like a playhouse. His company named their theatre 'The Globe'. A theme explored many times in Shakespeare's works is whether we are all like actors in a play. Disguise and deception, playing a part, directing the action: such theatrical conventions are also part of everyday experience. Like actors, people in real life are often not what they appear to be. Maybe you've met an Autolycus or a Perdita. And although, like Leontes, people may believe themselves to be in control of things because they have authority, they discover to their cost and humiliation that the action is shaped by a greater intelligence than they realised or were prepared to acknowledge. When Hamlet affirms, 'There's a divinity which shapes our ends, rough-hew them how we will' (V.2.10–11), he is voicing a wisdom achieved by a number of Shakespearean characters as they learn from experience the limits of human power and the surprisingly humane kindness of Providence.

In *The Winter's Tale*, Shakespeare develops a notion of Fortune which comes originally from the Roman philosopher Boethius's *Consolation of Philosophy* (AD523). Rather than a fickle goddess who randomly allocates good and bad luck on the deserving and undeserving alike, Fortune is shown to be part of a caring Providential mechanism. So, like Gonzalo at the end of *The Tempest* (V.I.205–13), in the final lines of *The Winter's Tale* (V.1.149–55) Leontes recognises Providential direction in the apparently chance series of terrible and wonderful events which have culminated in Perdita's marriage to Florizel and the union of two kingdoms. An action in which each of the principal characters has his/her 'part / Performed' (V.3.154–5).

JUSTICE, REPENTANCE, FORGIVENESS AND GRACE

Another theme which preoccupied Shakespeare throughout his career was the nature of true Justice, human and divine. The primitive code of 'an eye for an eye, a tooth for a tooth' powers the action of his first great tragedy, *Titus Andronicus*, a bloody revenge play which belongs more to the world of ancient Rome than Elizabethan England. Later, in *Measure for Measure* (1604), Shakespeare shows how without mercy, justice is approximate, ridiculous and barbarous. As Portia puts it in *The Merchant of Venice* (1596) 'The quality of mercy is not strained; / It droppeth as the gentle rain from heaven' (V.1.183–4). If we are to be worthy of God's grace, we must show mercy too.

In *The Winter's Tale*, again Shakespeare compels us to think about what we understand by Justice. Leontes's wild behaviour causes immense suffering. The innocent and decent Mamillius and Antigonus die directly as a result of his tyrannous actions and his refusal to heed the Oracle. Hermione loses her daughter and her life as Queen for sixteen years, Paulina loses her husband. The kingdom suffers too. Sicilia is 'heirless' for a generation, its future uncertain.

But it is Leontes's suffering, his 'saint-like sorrow' (V.1.2) which is foregrounded. And finally the broken king is rewarded for his genuine humility and long contrition by the miraculous restoration of his daughter, reunion with the friend he had wrongfully accused and what is like a second marriage to the wife whose true worth he has come to appreciate. If 'the heavens ... / ... strike at [his] injustice' (II.2.145–6), sixteen years later the heavens do indeed 'forget [his] evil' and 'forgive' Leontes (V.1.5–6). Leontes's recovery and the strengthening of both kingdoms by Perdita's marriage to Florizel is something denied his forebears in Shakespeare's great tragedies. It feels like something miraculous, the mature Shakespeare's affirmation that the universe is a benign place.

King Lear, with whom the rash Leontes has perhaps most in common, pays for the casting away of his innocent daughter by suffering through seeing her hanged, even though, like Leontes, he has finally realised her worth and repented his cruel folly. Lear dies of a broken heart and the mood at the end of that play is as bleak as anything seen on the English stage. Plato argued in *The Republic* (*c*.380BC) that Justice was giving people what they deserved. King Lear protests he is a man 'more sinned against than sinning'. It is a judgement only the stoniest hearted Pharisee would quarrel with.

The question arises whether in *The Winter's Tale* and the other late plays Shakespeare presents a modified tragic pattern which we find more satisfying, more just. Blindness, not viciousness, leads to sin. A terrible crisis leads to clear-sightedness, repentance, suffering, purification, redemption and finally to reconciliation, forgiveness, a new beginning and undreamed of happiness. In these late plays, the sentimental pessimism of *King Lear* (1605) gives way to life-belief.

LOYALTY AND SERVICE

The rights of Kings to be obeyed, even when their behaviour is despicable, exercised Shakespeare and his contemporaries; just forty years after the first performance of *The Winter's Tale*, the English Civil War culminated in the beheading of a King who believed he could defy Parliament.

Leontes and Polixenes are not just Kings but husbands and fathers too. One of the themes explored in the play is the proper relationship between those in authority and their subordinates. The play is remarkable for the episodes presenting Camillo, Hermione, Paulina, Perdita, Florizel and Leontes's courtiers as at the same time utterly loyal and verbally deferential whilst uncompromising in their refusal to submit to tyranny and nonsense. The exchanges are more realistic than those between King Lear and his minions because Shakespeare shows that Leontes and Polixenes are aware that no one gets away with tyranny. They threaten violence but, unlike Lear, compromise before doing others and themselves irreparable damage.

Camillo and Paulina like Kent in *King Lear* are selfless servants of the crown who bravely challenge their terrible master for his own good. What is interesting is that unlike Kent, Paulina and Camillo are not only rewarded for their dogged integrity but the play concludes with Paulina leading the whole company off stage, a **symbolic** affirmation of the principles she has championed since her first appearance on stage.

THE TRIUMPH OF TIME

Robert Greene's novel on which Shakespeare's play is closely based is called *Pandosto, or The Triumph of Time*. It was written in 1588 and may well have been in Shakespeare's mind many years a-maturing before he got round to turning it into a play. For example, Cordelia's ringing certainty, 'Time shall unfold what plighted cunning hides' (*King Lear*, I.2.279) may be an echo of *Pandosto*. These are the sentiments of Time the Chorus who appears in Act IV Scene 1. Students who know Shakespeare's play well, will learn a great deal about Shakespeare's methods by comparing Greene's novel and Shakespeare's re-presentation of it. You will find it printed as an appendix to the Signet, Arden and Oxford editions of the play (see Note on the Text).

In *The Winter's Tale*, we are encouraged to compare the progress of the seasons with the stages of human life, to see children as the continuation of their parents, to explore the relationship between death and birth and to observe how Time 'makes' and 'unfolds error' (IV.1.2). Time heals and allows people second chances. That which has been lost can be found. What we see in this play is, in T.S. Eliot's words, that 'Time the destroyer is time the preserver' (*The Dry Savages*, Faber & Faber, 1941, line 115).

CHILDREN AND CHILDHOOD

In *The Winter's Tale* Shakespeare explores the theme of childhood in two distinct ways. On the one hand, real children – Mamillius, Florizel and Perdita – are presented to us as possessing admirable, healthy qualities which promise well for the future. In the overall scheme of things, the sins of the fathers are purged by the virtues of their offspring. Florizel and Perdita achieve by marrying what Romeo and Juliet could achieve only by dying: reconciliation and hope for a better tomorrow. Tragically, like Romeo and Juliet, Mamillius pays for the sins of the father.

Mamillius is introduced by Archidamus as 'a gentleman / of the greatest promise' (I.1.34–5). Although he is a child, he is anything but coy or 'innocent'. Like the young Macduff, (*Macbeth*, Act IV Scene 2) he is an engaging, lively child who promises to become a shrewd adult which is what makes his death so distressing. Significantly, he has studied women's faces (II.1.12).

On the other hand, we have the Kings' attitude to their own childhoods and hence, adulthoods, which is presented to us as something unhealthy and disturbing. In the conversation which opens the play, Leontes and Polixenes are introduced as 'brothers'; as children they were brought up together. Camillo remarks that maturity brought 'separation' (I.1.25) of these childhood chums. Yet in the same speech it becomes clear that, in the psychological sense of the word, they have never 'separated': 'they have seemed to be / together, though absent; shook hands as over a vast; / and embraced, as it were, from the ends of opposed / winds' (I.1.28–31). Shakespeare is always interested in the consequences of excess. Although these images sound positive and could suggest a strong, mature, enduring friendship, on reflection we realise they imply something immature, even regressive in both men. When we consider the other details which Camillo gives us, 'interchange of gifts, / letters, loving embassies' (I.1.27–8) we begin to sense something overdone and inappropriate here. Where can the Kings' feelings for their wives fit in with all this?

This hint of something unhealthy in the two Kings' attachment to each other is immediately amplified when we learn that Polixenes having been on a visit for nine months in Sicilia, Leontes already plans to return the visit 'this coming Summer' (I.1.5). Polixenes has come without his wife and son; Leontes will leave his family behind.

But it is in Polixenes's conversation with Hermione (I.2.63ff) that the impression of something morbid in the Kings' attitude to their childhoods is confirmed. Polixenes remembers himself and Leontes as exchanging 'innocence for innocence'. Growing up he associates with learning 'the doctrine of ill-doing'. With sexual maturity has come the sense of sin. Hermione, alert to where this is leading, helps Polixenes to make his point explicit: 'By this we gather / You have tripped since' (I.2.75–6). And suddenly there it is, in the open. Sexual love, marriage, adulthood, parenting, far from being seen as healthy development are associated for Polixenes with 'temptations' and the fall from grace. Polixenes and Leontes, would have preferred to remain 'boy eternal' (I.2.65).

Instead of seeing growing up as leading one towards maturity, self-control, knowledge, wisdom and the joys of family life, it represents a decline from a natural innocence. Both Kings talk about their sons in enthusiastic terms, but it seems to be as reminders of the boys they were rather than as people with their own personalities that they regard them. Hermione effectively terminates Polixenes's unsavoury line of thought by making a joke of it 'Grace to boot! / ... devils' (I.2.80–2). It is precisely at this moment that Leontes comes within earshot and develops in his own grotesque way an attitude to woman as devil incubated by his 'brother'.

STRUCTURE OF THE PLAY

In the past, there was much criticism of Shakespeare having written a play with a sixteen year gap in the middle of it. Perhaps it's worth considering why it is such a good idea. After all, it is something we are used to today. It happens often in films.

Shakespeare was aware that he was violating the **classical unities** when he wrote *The Winter's Tale*. We know that because in *The Tempest* (1611), a play which has some striking thematic similarities to *The Winter's Tale*, he shaped his material very differently. In that play, the unities of time, place and action are more or less observed: the whole action occupies only as much time as it takes to perform. But for all its beauties, *The Tempest* is not an unblemished theatrical masterpiece and lacks something which makes the earlier play a more substantial dramatic experience.

In both plays, there has to be time for the lost princess to grow to marriageable age. In *The Tempest* Shakespeare dedicates most of the long first act to a series of contrived narratives which give the audience the necessary background to the events about to be presented on stage. These narratives contain some of Shakespeare's most accomplished verse. But they work better on the page than on the stage and often make the audience restless.

But the chief loss in *The Tempest* is that by presenting the first half of the drama through narrative, Shakespeare does not allow us to *see* what happened in the past, to *see* the effects of Time on the principal characters. There is all the difference in the world between being told that Miranda was just a baby when her wicked Uncle committed her to the savage mercies of the elements and *seeing* baby Perdita narrowly escape being devoured by a bear and *hearing* the merciless storm which is her 'lullaby' (III.3.54). Even more important is *seeing* how sixteen years have changed Leontes, Polixenes, Hermione, Camillo, Paulina and Perdita, *seeing* what Time does to people, taking them through the different stages of life.

The grey-haired Leontes new-wooing and embracing the '*wrinkled*' (V.3.28) Hermione, being thrilled that although she's older, she's still 'warm' (V.3.109) is as an important part of the theatrical effect as is the common-place wonder of *seeing* the discarded baby the Shepherd picked up grown into the captivating young woman who is Perdita.

IMAGERY

Much of the power of Shakespeare's verse comes from the great number and variety of pictures-in-words he paints. His characters express themselves graphically; there is little abstract language.

We are given strong mental pictures of the present and the particular. For example, vivid imagery works on the audience's imaginary forces when the Clown describes the terrible storm which destroys the boat which brought Antigonus and Perdita to the shores of Bohemia: 'now the ship boring / the moon with her mainmast, and anon swallowed with / yest and froth, as you'd thrust a cork into a hogs-head / ... to see how the sea flap-dragoned it' (III.3.89–95). Similarly concrete are the Clown's and the Shepherd's acute observations of Autolycus: 'His garments are rich, but he wears them not / handsomely / ... He seems ... noble ... / ... I know by the picking / on's teeth' (IV.4.745–9) and the servant's inventory of Autolycus's wares: 'ribbons of all the colours i'th'rainbow; / points ... / ... inkles, caddisses, cambrics, lawns' (IV.4.206–9). Equally characteristic is Shakespeare's delight in figurative language. The courtier compares the Old Shepherd to 'a weather-bitten conduit of many kings' reigns' (V.2.54); Florizel describes the dancing Perdita to 'A wave o'th'sea' (IV.4.141) and Leontes tells us Camillo's acute mind is 'soaking, will draw in / More than the common blocks'

(I.2.224–5). Abstract ideas are made graphic. Despairing of women's chastity, Leontes proclaims: 'Be it concluded, / No barricado for a belly. Know't; / It will let in and out the enemy / With bag and baggage' (I.2.203–6) and sleeplessness is 'spotted' sheets which are 'goads, thorns, nettles, tails of wasps' (I.2.328–9). Polixenes imagines his son's rustic seductress working like a canny fisherman, 'I / fear, the angle that plucks our son thither' (IV.2.44–5) recalling Leontes's paranoid fantasy that he's one of those whose wives have been 'sluiced in's absence, / And his pond fished by his next neighbour, by / Sir Smile, his neighbour (I.2.194–6). This vivid, pictorial way of working on the audience's imagination is characteristic of Shakespeare's verse generally. What gives *The Winter's Tale* its particular tone is the nature of many of the most powerful images in the play. Whereas in *Hamlet*, much of the imagery paints pictures of *corruption and disease*, in *The Winter's Tale*, what's striking are the number of images associated with *disease and cure, medicine and recovery*.

The two Kings are associated explicitly with liability to disease. Leontes, lost in jealousy, declares his sickness to be universal: 'Physic for't there's none: / … Many thousands on's / Have the disease' (I.2.200–7). Camillo tactfully unfolding to Polixenes the hideous state of affairs in which unwittingly he is embroiled says, 'There is a sickness / Which puts some of us in distemper but / I cannot name the disease; and it is caught / Of you, that yet are well' (I.2.384–7). In the lines which follow, the conceit is developed. Polixenes likes to think of his looks as promoting health not, like the basilisk's, infection (I.2.388). When Camillo reveals the shocking truth, again Polixenes uses disease imagery: 'O, then my best blood turn / To an infected jelly … / … my freshest reputation to / A savour that may strike the dullest nostril / Where I arrive, and my approach be shunned, / Nay, hated too, worse than the great'st infection / That e'er was heard or read!' (I.2.417–24).

This is something more than a colourful way of speaking. Throughout the play, Camillo and Paulina's describe their role as being counsellor-priest-physician to the Kings. And this is how their function is perceived by others. The deluded Leontes describes his erupting jealousy as '*tremor cordis*' (I.2.110) and feels 'the infection of my brains' (I.2.145). He appeals to Camillo like this: 'I have trusted thee, Camillo, / With all the nearest things to my heart … / … wherein, priestlike, thou / Hast cleansed my bosom, I have from thee departed / Thy penitent

reformed' (I.2.235–9). As Leontes's 'distemper' (I.2.385) becomes
manifest, Camillo's words sound like those of an exorcist: 'Good my lord,
be cured / Of this diseased opinion, and betimes, / For 'tis most
dangerous' (I.2.296–8). Mad, Leontes attempts to fasten the imagery on
his unsullied wife: 'Were my wife's liver / Infected as her life, she would
not live / The running of one glass' (I.2.304–6). Camillo takes up the
conceit: 'Who does infect her?' (I.2.306). The remedy Leontes proposes
is for Camillo, the restorative cup-bearer to administer poison, a draft
Leontes fondly believes would cure him: 'Which draught to me were
cordial' (I.2.18).

Camillo, in his role as physician, cannily replies: 'I am his
cup-bearer. / If from me he hath wholesome beverage, / Account me not
your servant' (I.2.345–7). He *will* administer that 'wholesome beverage'
in advising Polixenes to flee Sicilia, and thus cease to be Leontes's servant
for the next sixteen years. Henceforth, whilst Camillo serves as
Polixenes's 'pilot' (I.2.448) his role as Leontes's doctor is taken over by
Paulina. In Act II Scene 3 she arrives to bring the insomniac 'sleep'
(II.3.33) 'with words as med'cinal as true' (II.3.37). When challenged by
Leontes she boldly announces herself allowed privileged access; she is his
'loyal servant ... physician / ... most obedient counsellor' (II.3.54–5). Her
diagnosis is presented in the language of a surgeon. Someone must
'remove / The root of his opinion, which is rotten' (II.3.88–9).
Forensically she hopes the baby's mind has 'No yellow in't' (II.3.106). As
she leaves the chamber, she protests the honesty of her mission, to 'do
him good' (II.3.128) which job the courtiers are too 'tender' to wield the
surgeon's steel. T.S. Eliot's phrase 'The sharp compassion of the healer's
art' (*East Coker*, Faber & Faber, 1940, line 150) fits perfectly the role
Paulina plays in the rest of the play.

The brief interlude between Cleomenes and Dion, establishes the
symbolic contrast between the unhealthy Sicilian court and the healthy
home of truth, Delphos, where 'The climate's delicate, the air most sweet,
/ Fertile' (III.1.1–2). Leontes says he hopes the trial will result in
'purgation' (II.2.7). When Hermione collapses in a dead faint, Leontes
begs his servants to 'tenderly apply ... / Some remedies for life'
(III.2.152–3).

And the children, too, are seen as agents in the healing process. At
the very beginning of the play, when Camillo is praising Mamillius, he

describes him as 'one that indeed physics the subject, / makes old hearts fresh' (I.1.37–8). But by Act II Scene 3, we hear that Mamillius is sick. His loss results in Sicilia becoming heirless, barren and wintry until his sister's and Florizel's visit is compared to the return of spring (V.1.151).

Asked about his relationship with his son, Polixenes tells us how 'with his varying childness [he] cures in me / Thoughts that would thick my blood' (I.2.170–1). But by Act IV Scene 2 it is Camillo who has been playing his chamber-counsellor for sixteen years. Florizel recognises Camillo as the 'Preserver of [his] father, now of [him], / The medicine of [their] house' (IV.4.584–5). We are reminded that when Camillo asked leave to return to Sicilia, Polixenes's alarm expressed itself in similar terms. If it is 'a sickness' to refuse him, it would be 'death' to grant him leave to go (IV.2.1–3). Yet Camillo wishes to return to his physician's role in Sicilia where be 'might be some allay' (IV.2.8) to his old master's suffering. Autolycus thinks he is lying, but when he tells the Shepherd that Polixenes has gone aboard a ship 'to purge melancholy' (IV.4.759) he is speaking more truth than he is aware of.

After the fresh air of the Bohemian scenes, the imagery of sickness and its cure returns as we revisit Sicilia. If Florizel's and Perdita's touch of sea-sickness (V.2.116–8) is charming, we are reminded of the soul-sickness which Leontes has been penitentially suffering for under the searching hands of Paulina. Leontes reminds us of his 'blemishes' (V.1.8) Paulina that the only 'remedy' (V.1.77) will be a second marriage to Hermione. The arrival of the couple will, Leontes hopes, persuade the gods to 'Purge all infection from our air whilst you / Do climate here' (V.1.168–9). The audience looks forward to the 'issueless' King being rewarded for his contrition.

The 'madness' and 'affliction' which Leontes receives at Paulina's medicinal hands in the final scene of the play (V.3.73–7) is paradoxically 'cordial comfort'. We cannot but remember the *'tremor cordis'* (I.2.110) which precipitated all the mischief.

PART FOUR

TEXTUAL ANALYSIS

TEXT 1   (I.2.108–46 AND I.2.185–208)

She [HERMIONE] *gives her hand to* POLIXENES

LEONTES: (*aside*)   Too hot, too hot!
To mingle friendship far is mingling bloods.
I have *tremor cordis* on me: my heart dances   110
But not for joy, not joy, This entertainment
May a free face put on, derive a liberty
From heartiness, from bounty, fertile bosom,
And well become the agent – 't may, I grant.
But to be paddling palms and pinching fingers   115
As now they are, and making practised smiles
As in a looking glass; and then to sigh, as 'twere
The mort o'th'deer – O, that is entertainment
My bosom likes not, nor my brows! Mamillius,
Art thou my boy?

MAMILLIUS: Ay, my good lord.

LEONTES: I'fecks!   120
Why, that's my bawcock. What, hast smutched thy
    nose?
They say it is a copy out of mine. Come, captain,
We must be neat – not neat but cleanly, captain.
And yet the steer, the heifer, and the calf
Are all called neat. Still virginalling   125
Upon his palm? – How now, you wanton calf!
Art thou my calf?

MAMILLIUS: Yes, if you will, my lord.

LEONTES: Thou want'st a rough pash and the shoots that I have
To be full like me; yet they say we are
Almost as like as eggs. Women say so,   130

That will say anything. But were they false
As o'er-dyed blacks, as wind, as waters, false
As dice are to be wished by one that fixes
No bourn 'twixt his and mine, yet were it true
To say this boy were like me. Come, sir page,   135
Look on me with your welkin eye. Sweet villain!
Most dear'st! My collop! Can thy dam? May't be?
Affection, thy intention stabs the centre.
Thou dost make possible things not so held,
Communicat'st with dreams – how can this be? –   140
With what's unreal thou coactive art,
And fellow'st nothing. Then 'tis very credent
Thou mayst co-join with something; and thou dost,
And that beyond commission, and I find it,
And that to the infection of my brains   145
And hardening of my brows.

Exeunt HERMIONE *and* POLIXENES
           Gone already!   185
Inch-thick, knee-deep, o'er head and ears a forked one!
Go play, boy, play: thy mother plays, and I
Play too – but so disgraced a part, whose issue
Will hiss me to my grave. Contempt and clamour
Will be my knell. Go play, boy, play. There have been,   190
Or I am much deceived, cuckolds ere now;
And many a man there is, even at this present,
Now, while I speak this, holds his wife by th'arm,
That little thinks she has been sluiced in's absence,
And his pond fished by his next neighbour, by   195
Sir Smile, his neighbour. Nay, there's comfort in't
Whiles other men have gates, and those gates opened,
As mine, against their will. Should all despair
That have revolted wives, the tenth of mankind
Would hang themselves. Physic for't there's none: 200
It is a bawdy planet, that will strike
Where 'tis predominant; and 'tis powerful, think it,

From east, west, north, and south. Be it concluded,
No barricado for a belly. Know't:
It will let in and out the enemy   205
With bag and baggage. Many thousand on's
Have the disease and feel't not. How now, boy?
MAMILLIUS: I am like you, they say.

Shakespeare frequently separates two parts of a single developing meditation to give it greater intensity for its interruption by a contrasting episode. Here, Leontes's disturbing reflections are made more sinister by the contrasting tone, **rhythm** and vocabulary of the reminiscences on childhood which he shares with Polixenes and Hermione.

At line 108, Leontes deliberately draws aside from Hermione and Polixenes to brood on his suspicions and to torture himself by watching them. It is at this point that his anxious insecurity explodes revealing all that has been pent up.

Playfully, Hermione accused Leontes of dealing 'too coldly' with his friend. Now Leontes's seething private jealousy erupts as a hideous counter-accusation. His wife's a whore: 'Too hot, too hot!'. Shakespeare captures Leontes's obsession partly through the use of repetitions. Some are packed closely together, generating a manic **ostinato**: 'mingle … mingling', 'not for joy, not joy', 'May … / … may', 'Come, captain / … captain', 'neat – not neat … / … called neat', 'calf / … calf / … calf', 'And that … / And that … / And'. Others work over a longer span, like a nagging musical refrain: 'like me … like me'.

Leontes's wild state of mind is also developed through the broken rhythms of the verse, and through expression which verges on the logically unintelligible, 'What means Sicilia?' asks Polixenes. Yet the emotional logic of these dark musings is sharply etched. Without a tempter, without provocation, without a grain of sense, Leontes wills himself into a passion which threatens to destroy everything in Sicilia. He is fascinated by the minute particulars he perceives through the distorting lens of his crazy eye: 'to be paddling palms … / … The mort o'th'deer … / … Still virginalling / Upon his palm'. What is important here is the contrast between what the audience sees and what Leontes says he sees. This is great drama. Because what the audience experiences in the first extract is, simultaneously, the sight of the uncomplicated, decent, open,

warm and spontaneously friendly body-language of Leontes's utterly
loyal, beautifully pregnant wife (the second-time audience knows it's
Leontes's delightful daughter inside her) talking unaffectedly to the
man who really is his best friend, and Leontes's mad commentary upon
it. It is a kind of psychological 'realism' unexplored with such intensity
much before the writings of Poe and Dostoyevsky and the paintings of
Edward Munch in the nineteenth century. We watch appalled, moved
but detached as we observe someone suffer cruelly and wholly
unnecessarily. The dramatic poignancy of this scene is intensified by the
presence on stage of the delightful Mamillius, the lovely child Leontes's
jealousy is going to destroy. Mamillius and his playful innocence are
introduced to the audience only so it can grieve at their needless sacrifice
on the altar of this father's wild egotism. As Leontes talks half to himself
and half to his son, Mamillius's puzzled, innocent responses highlight the
contrast of his father's sordid thoughts. His crazy jealous musings
counterpointed by a wild possessiveness allow of no easy communication,
no genuine conversation between father and son, a diseased adult and a
child desperate to please him. Each time we hear the word 'play' the
contrast between vulnerable innocence and dangerous delusion is
intensified.

Leontes orders Hermione: 'How thou lov'st us show in our
brother's welcome' (line 174). As she leaves with Polixenes, Leontes
describes himself as 'angling' (line 180). Voyeuristically, he sets up the
situation to confirm his suspicions. In this extract, Shakespeare plays a
trick on the audience which watched the frenzied Leontes in his first
outburst with easy critical detachment. Leontes's suspicions have moved
from the awakenings of jealousy into the conviction of his being a
ludicrous cuckold. Leontes's insecurity now turns into a wholesale
distrust of women. Absolutely out of his mind, what gives him
paradoxical comfort is the idea that he is not alone: 'And many a man
there is ... / ... Sir Smile, his neighbour'. Suddenly, as Leontes addresses
the audience directly, the husbands that came to the theatre as trusting
friends begin perhaps to entertain just the flickerings of a doubt which
threatens to shove them from their comfortable critical stance as
Leontes's bemused spectators to wonder if just possibly they might be his
fellows, entertaining what Macbeth describes as 'saucy doubts and fears'.
A skilful actor can play this moment of humour which is the other side

of horror and draw the nervous smile from the stalls, cause a few palms to perspire.

There is much more in the language to relish. For example, the tactile mimetic effect of the phrase 'paddling palms and pinching fingers'; the sounds of hissing sibilants which catch the note of fascinated disgust and animate the graphic imagery in 'thinks **she** has been **sl**uiced in's absence, / And his pond fished by his next neighbour, by / Sir Smile'.

TEXT 2 (IV.4.55–129)

Enter SHEPHERD, *with* POLIXENES *and* CAMILLO, *disguised;* CLOWN, MOPSA, DORCAS, *and others*

SHEPHERD: Fie, daughter! When my old wife lived, upon   55
This day she was both pantler, butler, cook;
Both dame and servant; welcomed all, served all;
Would sing her song and dance her turn; now here,
At upper end o'th'table, now i'th'middle;
On his shoulder, and his; her face o'fire   60
With labour, and the thing she took to quench it:
She would to each one sip. You are retired,
As if you were a feasted one and not
The hostess of the meeting. Pray you, bid
These unknown friends to's welcome, for it is   65
A way to make us better friends, more known.
Come, quench your blushes and present yourself
That which you are, Mistress o'th'Feast. Come on,
And bid us welcome to your sheep-shearing,
As your good flock shall prosper.

PERDITA: (*to* POLIXENES)   Sir, welcome.   70
It is my father's will I should take on me
The hostess-ship o'th'day. (*To* CAMILLO) You're welcome,
    sir.
Give me those flowers there, Dorcas. Reverend sirs,
For you there's rosemary and rue; these keep
Seeming and savour all the winter long: 75

Grace and remembrance be to you both,
And welcome to our shearing!

POLIXENES: Shepherdess –
A fair one are you – well you fit our ages
With flowers of winter.

PERDITA: Sir, the year growing ancient,
Not yet on summer's death nor on the birth   80
Of trembling winter, the fairest flowers o'th'season
Are our carnations and streaked gillyvors,
Which some call Nature's bastards; of that kind
Our rustic garden's barren, and I care not
To get slips of them.

POLIXENES: Wherefore, gentle maiden,   85
Do you neglect them?

PERDITA: For I have heard it said
There is art which in their piedness shares
With great creating Nature.

POLIXENES: Say there be;
Yet Nature is made better by no mean
But Nature makes that mean; so over that art   90
Which you say adds to Nature is an art
That Nature makes. You see, sweet maid, we marry
A gentler scion to the wildest stock,
And make conceive a bark of baser kind
By bud of nobler race. This is an art   95
Which does mend Nature – change it, rather – but
The art itself is Nature.

PERDITA: So it is.

POLIXENES: Then make your garden rich in gillyvors,
And do not call them bastards.

PERDITA: I'll not put
The dibble in earth to set one slip of them: 100
No more than, were I painted, I would wish

This youth should say 'twere well, and only therefore
Desire to breed by me. Here's flowers for you:
Hot lavender, mints, savory, marjoram;
The marigold, that goes to bed with' sun   105
And with him rises weeping; these are flowers
Of middle summer, and I think they are given
To men of middle age. Y'are very welcome.
CAMILLO: I should leave grazing, were I of your flock,
Add only live by gazing.

PERDITA: Out, alas!   110
You'd be so lean that blasts of January
Would blow you through and through. (*To* FLORIZEL)
       Now, my fair'st friend,
I would I had some flowers o'th'spring, that might
Become your time of day – (*to the* SHEPHERDESSES) and
       yours, and yours,
That wear upon your virgin branches yet   115
Your maidenheads growing. O Proserpina,
For the flowers now that, frighted, thou let'st fall
From Dis's wagon! Daffodils,
That come before the swallow dares, and take
The winds of March with beauty; violets, dim,   120
But sweeter than the lids of Juno's eyes
Or Cytherea's breath; pale primroses,
That die unmarried ere they can behold
Bright Phoebus in his strength – a malady
Most incident to maids; bold oxlips and   125
The crown imperial; lilies of all kinds,
The flower-de-luce being one: O, these I lack
To make you garlands of, and my sweet friend
To strew him o'er and o'er!

This passage is remarkable for the way Shakespeare weaves together in
such a short space, seamlessly and with apparent naturalness, a rich
variety of dramatic purposes and poetic styles.

The delightful narrative portrait of his wife painted by the
Shepherd has a Chaucerian comic vitality. She is the fourth strong

woman in this play, revered by her husband. We don't notice that this rustic who usually speaks in **prose** now speaks in **blank verse** because these lines are so vigorous, so flexible, so close to the rhythms of **colloquial** speech, the **diction** so unmistakably the Shepherd's own. This isn't the stilted stuff of courtly **pastoral**, it is insistently concrete. In Robert Greene's *Pandosto* (1588), the Shepherd's wife is present; Shakespeare makes her a much more vivid character by presenting her as she lives in her fond husband's memory. The portrait is full of movement; his sprightly, accomplished wife thrived on cheerful, generous business:

> she was both pantler, butler, cook,
> Both dame and servant; welcomed all, served all,
> Would sing her song and dance her turn; now here
> ... now i'th' middle;
> On his shoulder, and his; ...
> ...
> She would to each one sip

We see her frozen momentarily as in a party snapshot: 'her face o'fire / With labour, and the thing she took to quench it' (lines 60–1).

And then we hear in the lines which follow the equally spirited, loving foster father (we'd never guess he was eighty-three!) who has done so much to nurture the robust Perdita who is about to engage Polixenes in a philosophical dispute: 'You are retired, / ... Pray you, bid / These unknown friends to's welcome ... / Come, quench your blushes and present yourself ... / Come on' (lines 63–8).

That 'pray you' captures delicately the old man's fond firmness with his bashful child and his instinctive respect for this foster daughter he loves and knows to be out of his class, not just because he discovered her with the credentials of a courtier's child but from his frank, daily delight in her many accomplishments (see lines 178–82). Among which is a confidence to engage a King (at least one in disguise) in a philosophical wrestle. To extract the Nature/Nurture debate as if it were some philosophical treatise Shakespeare were contributing to is to misrepresent grievously his way of working. Something everyone is fascinated by, today, as for thousands of years, is the extent to which personalities are the product of genes and/or upbringing (i.e. the product of Nature or Nurture). And in these late plays Shakespeare gives us plenty to reflect

upon. Like Miranda in *The Tempest* (1611), Perdita has grown up far
away from court. Like Miranda, she speaks with a natural poise, a verbal
sophistication quite unlike her foster brother's, and with a degree of
education which might not be expected in one brought up in a sheepcote.
But unlike Miranda, her father for the last sixteen years has not been her
natural father or a schoolmaster with a library. And yet, engaging
Polixenes in debate, Perdita uses an argument from the same essay by
Montaigne (*Essaies*, 1595) as Shakespeare plays with in *The Tempest*, and
she knows (see below) her Ovid well too.

But that isn't something we would know if scholars hadn't pointed
it out. What the audience hears isn't 'bookish theoric' but a lively, active
intelligence. Explaining her moral repugnance with plants produced by
genetic engineering, she tells Polixenes: 'I have heard … / There is an art
which in their piedness shares / With great creating Nature' (lines 86–8).
She follows Polixenes's interesting counterargument but brusquely
washes her hands of it as so much ingenious sophistry: 'I'll not put / The
dibble in earth to set one slip of them' (lines 99–100). Her objection is
not a logical but a moral one: 'No more than, were I painted, I would
wish / This youth should say 'twere well, and only therefore / Desire to
breed by me' (lines 101–3). The 'dibble' makes her sounds plausibly like
the one who does the gardening; the refusal to compromise on so
important a moral issue unmistakably Hermione's daughter. And she can
sense, perhaps, that this speaker who maintains so rationally that 'we
marry / A gentler scion to the wildest stock, / And make conceive a bark
of baser kind / By bud of nobler race' (lines 92–5) when it comes to the
crunch, will show that he doesn't believe a word of what he elegantly
professes. A great deal depends on the tone of voice in which the actress
delivers the words, 'So it is'. (line 97). Given Perdita's well-founded fears
of what Florizel's father will say when he discovers what his son is up to,
perhaps she suspects this radical argument is a trap. That the mysterious
stranger is one of the King's spies playing devil's advocate. We already
know (from Act IV Scene 2) and will shortly see again that Polixenes is
horrified that 'a sceptre's heir, / … affects a sheep-hook!' (lines 416–17).
For Perdita to agree with his revolutionary argument might be signing
her death warrant.

The other voice we hear in this extract is Perdita's lyrical
assumption of the role of Flora, goddess of flowers and fertility, of whom

Proserpina was an earlier manifestation. In recalling that other lost child whose recovery restores fertility to the earth, Perdita sounds less like someone who has read the story in Ovid's *Metamorphoses* (*c*. 8AD) than the latest incarnation of the undying spirit of regeneration. When Leontes welcomes his daughter back to Sicilia, he will stumble to know what to make of her 'fair princess – goddess!' (V.1.130). The couple's arrival will be as 'Welcome ... / As is the spring to th'earth' (V.1.150–1). Again, Shakespeare delicately blends **realism** and **symbolism** and we murder the play to disunite the two. Elizabethan **iconography** is notoriously imprecise. The precise significance of each of the flowers in Perdita's catalogue is less important than the sense of glorious, colourful, fragrant abundance which the speech evokes.

TEXT 3   (IV.4.388–463)

POLIXENES: Soft, swain, awhile, beseech you.
Have you a father?

FLORIZEL: I have; but what of him?

POLIXENES: Knows he of this?

FLORIZEL: He neither does nor shall.   390

POLIXENES: Methinks a father
Is at the nuptial of his son a guest
That best becomes the table. Pray you once more,
Is not your father grown incapable
Of reasonable affairs? Is he not stupid   395
With age and altering rheums? Can he speak? Hear?
Know man from man? Dispute his own estate?
Lies he not bed-rid? And again does nothing
But what he did being childish?

FLORIZEL: No, good sir:
He has his health, and ampler strength indeed   400
Than most have of his age.

POLIXENES: By my white beard,

You offer him, if this be so, a wrong
Something unfilial. Reason my son
Should choose himself a wife, but as good reason
The father, all whose joy is nothing else   405
But fair posterity, should hold some counsel
In such a business.

FLORIZEL: I yield all this;
But for some other reasons, my grave sir,
Which 'tis not fit you know, I not acquaint
My father of this business.

POLIXENES: Let him know't.   410

FLORIZEL: He shall not.

POLIXENES: Prithee, let him.

FLORIZEL: No, he must not.

SHEPHERD: Let him, my son: he shall not need to grieve
At knowing of thy choice.

FLORIZEL: Come, come, he must not.
Mark our contract.

POLIXENES: (*removing his disguise*) Mark your divorce,
     young sir,
Whom son I dare not call: thou art too base   415
To be acknowledged. Thou a sceptre's heir,
That thus affects a sheep-hook? – Thou, old traitor,
I am sorry that by hanging thee I can
But shorten thy life one week. – And thou, fresh piece
Of excellent witchcraft, who of force must know   420
The royal fool thou cop'st with –

SHEPHERD: O, my heart!

POLIXENES: I'll have thy beauty scratched with briers and made
More homely than thy state. – For thee, fond boy,
If I may ever know thou dost but sigh
That thou no more shalt see this knack – as never   425
I mean thou shalt – we'll bar thee from succession;

Not hold thee of our blood, no, not our kin,
Far than Deucalion off. Mark thou my words!
Follow us to the court. – Thou, churl, for this time,
Though full of our displeasure, yet we free thee   430
From the dead blow of it. – And you, enchantment,
Worthy enough a herdsman – yea, him too,
That makes himself, but for our honour therein,
Unworthy thee – if ever henceforth thou
These rural latches to his entrance open,   435
Or hoop his body more with thy embraces,
I will devise a death as cruel for thee
As thou art tender to't.

Exit

PERDITA: Even here undone!
I was not much afeard; for once or twice
I was about to speak and tell him plainly,   440
The selfsame sun that shines upon his court
Hides not his visage from our cottage, but
Looks on alike. (*To* FLORIZEL) Will't please you, sir, be
     gone?
I told you what would come of this. Beseech you,
Of your own state take care. This dream of mine –   445
Being now awake, I'll queen it no inch farther,
But milk my ewes, and weep.

CAMILLO: Why, how now, father!
Speak ere thou die'st.

SHEPHERD: I cannot speak nor think,
Nor dare to know that which I know. (*To* FLORIZEL) O sir!
You have undone a man of fourscore three,   450
That thought to fill his grave in quiet, yea,
To die upon the bed my father died,
To live close by his honest bones; but now
Some hangman must put on my shroud and lay me
Where no priest shovels in dust. (*To* PERDITA) O cursed
     wretch,   455

That knew'st this was the Prince and wouldst adventure
To mingle faith with him! Undone, undone!
If I might die within this hour, I have lived
To die when I desire.

Exit

FLORIZEL: Why look you so upon me?
I am but sorry, not afeard; delayed,   460
But nothing altered: what I was I am;
More straining on for plucking back, not following
My leash unwillingly.

We, the audience, have seen enough to convince us that Florizel and
Perdita are in love and are worthy of one another; we also know that their
union will unite the two kingdoms and complete the dramatic and moral
pattern of the play. This places us in an interesting dramatic relationship
to the King who has all of the first half but none of the second half of that
knowledge.

Although it is neither as morbid nor as destructive in its
consequences as Leontes's, there is a vicious edge and a degree of
psychological penetration in Shakespeare's presentation of Polixenes's
rude interruption of the natural pairing and healing processes which
reminds us of where we have been, of the emotional territory the play has
covered in the previous two hours. Both Kings' tantrums are examples of
Everyman's capacity for a heady unreasonableness which, unchecked, can
result in incalculable suffering. Polixenes's outburst is less disturbing than
Leontes's mania because Shakespeare doesn't develop it (he takes
Polixenes off the stage, not, as in Act I Scene 2, the objects of the King's
distemper). And having shared Time's perspective on things, the
audience senses a pattern rolling along towards a prosperous conclusion
which Polixenes's outburst can't possibly arrest; the energy, the vitality we
have enjoyed in this scene is substantial not the mere semblance of
prosperity with which the play began. Polixenes's waspishness cannot but
be incorporated into the sweep of restoration Leontes's painful years of
penitence are paying for.

Yet when it comes, like a storm rudely interrupting the celebration
of the sheep-shearing and the rural-royal couple's betrothal, Shakespeare
gives Polixenes's outburst just enough genuine nastiness and excessive

cruelty to disturb the audience, to make it examine the nature of his objections to a match which, theoretically, he seemed to recommend earlier in the scene (lines 92–5).

In their only conversation in the play, Polixenes and Florizel speak to one another with a degree of formality which barely disguises their mutual asperity. Whatever the truth of the King's account of how he and his son related sixteen years ago (I.2.165–71) what we witness here suggests there's little fondness now. If Polixenes is understandably appalled at the notion of an alliance between a prince and a shepherdess, what infuriates him is the lack of warmth for his father which Florizel betrays in the lines leading up to the rupture. There is a reverberation of the odd attitude to Childhood (see Theme on Children and Childhood) which the King expressed in Act I Scene 2, in the way he reacts when his son dares to state honestly the blunt fact that 'one dead' he will be King. It is as if Polixenes feels the operations of Time should be denied. Polixenes is nettled: 'Is ... your father grown incapable ... what he did being childish?' (lines 394–9). Not that Polixenes is geriatric; Florizel is quick to defend him against these exaggerations, 'He hath his health and ampler strength indeed / Than most have of his age' (lines 400–1). But the fact of Polixenes's 'age' remains; Shakespeare has taken considerable trouble to show us that the King and his peers are not the vigorous young people they were in Act I: ageing is a fact of life which this play deliberately draws attention to. Perdita having already upset Polixenes by spontaneously offering him winter flowers (lines 74–5) tactfully adjusted the bouquet to suit a man of 'middle age' (lines 103–8). But Polixenes belongs to that lineage of jealous fathers who wish to control their children when it is beginning to be both unreasonable and unseemly for them to do so. Although he can *talk* about 'The father, all whose joy is nothing else / But fair posterity' (IV.4.405–6) he doesn't *feel* it. Recognising a child's sexuality and his/her right to independence is a complicated adjustment. It involves acknowledging that one is losing 'potency' in many senses of the word.

Something which the late plays have in common is a wisdom which recognises that the greatest joy of old age is embracing the new role of being a grandparent, entering the third age, abdicating, letting go joyfully. Paulina guides Leontes through the process of embracing age in the prelude to the restoration in Act V.

Here, Polixenes overreacts, condemning the kindly, wholly innocent shepherd to hanging and, even more disturbingly turns on Perdita: 'I'll have thy beauty scratched with briers' (line 422). But what reminds us of Leontes's wildness is this: 'we'll bar thee from succession; / ... Far than Deucalion off' (lines 426–8). For a moment he sounds like King Lear disowning Cordelia. And Polixenes has no other children. What is he contemplating doing to his kingdom? It is the intensity of his passion which we register, not the merits of the case. It is over in a minute, Polixenes no sooner condemns the innocent to their vile punishments than he commutes their sentences (lines 433–8) and Camillo's agenda and the couple's constancy quickly conspire to outmanoeuvre his loud attempt to 'divorce' (line 414) his son and Perdita. It is a curious example of Shakespeare wanting to have the best of both worlds that neither the Shepherd nor Camillo hears Polixenes's pardon (lines 447–58). At the same time that we are relieved that this is just a storm in a teacup, we register that it is something with as hideously destructive a potential as Leontes's mad jealousy.

PART FIVE

Background

Shakespeare's life

There are no personal records of Shakespeare's life. Official documents and occasional references to him by contemporaries enable us to draw the main outline of his public life, but his private life remains hidden. Although not at all unusual for a writer of his time, this lack of first-hand evidence has tempted many to read his plays as personal records and to look in them for clues to Shakespeare's own character and convictions. The results are unconvincing, partly because Renaissance art was not subjective or designed primarily to express the creator's personality, and partly because the drama of any period is very difficult to read biographically. Except when plays are written by committed dramatists to promote social or political causes (as by Shaw or Brecht), it is all but impossible to decide who amongst the variety of fictional characters in a drama represents the dramatist, or which of the various and often conflicting points of view expressed is authorial. *Measure for Measure*'s insistence on raising questions and dramatising opposing viewpoints makes any attempt to deduce Shakespeare's own feelings about his subject matter hopeless.

What we do know about Shakespeare's life can be quickly summarised. Shakespeare was born into a well-to-do family in the market town of Stratford-upon-Avon in Warwickshire in 1564, and was baptised in the town's Holy Trinity Church on 26 April. His father, John Shakespeare, was a prosperous glover and leather merchant who became a person of some importance in the town: in 1565 he was elected an alderman and in 1568 he became high bailiff, or mayor of Stratford. He married Mary Arden in 1557, and William was the third of their eight children and their eldest son. It seems probable that William went to the local grammar school where he, like all Elizabethan schoolboys, would have studied a curriculum of Latin, history, logic and rhetoric. In November 1582, when he was aged eighteen, William married Anne Hathaway, who was twenty-six. The birth of their first daughter, Susanna, six months later in May 1983, suggests either that the couple married in haste when they learned of Anne's pregnancy or that there was some kind of civil contract before the marriage ceremony. Twins, Hamnet and Judith, were born to the marriage in 1585.

Shakespeare next appears in the historical record in 1592 when he is mentioned as a London actor and playwright by the dramatist Robert Greene. These 'lost years' 1585–92 have been the subject of much speculation, but how they were occupied remains as much of a mystery as when Shakespeare left Stratford and why. In his pamphlet, *Greene's Groatsworth of Wit*, Greene expresses to his fellow dramatists his outrage that the 'upstart crow' Shakespeare has the impudence to believe he 'is as well able to bombast out a blank verse as the best of you'. To have aroused this hostility from a rival, Shakespeare must, by 1592, have been long enough in London to have made a name for himself as a playwright. We may conjecture that he had left Stratford in 1586 or 1587.

During the next twenty years, Shakespeare continued to live in London, presumably visiting his wife and family in Stratford. He continued to act, but his chief fame was as a dramatist. From 1594 he wrote exclusively for the Lord Chamberlain's Men which rapidly became the leading dramatic company and from 1603 enjoyed to patronage of James I as the King's Men. His plays were popular and he became a shareholder in the profitable theatre company, earning enough money to buy land and a large house in Stratford. He retired to his home town in about 1611, and died there on 23 April 1616. He was buried in Holy Trinity Church.

SHAKESPEARE'S DRAMATIC CAREER

Between the late 1580s and 1613 Shakespeare wrote thirty-seven plays and contributed to some by other dramatists. This was by no means an exceptional number for a professional playwright of the times, particularly in the context of a theatre industry which was hungry for new plays, each of which would probably have fewer than ten performances. The exact date of the composition of individual plays is a matter of debate – for only a few plays is the date of their first performance known – but the broad outlines of Shakespeare's dramatic career have been established. He began in the late 1580s and early 1590s with **comedies**, such as *The Comedy of Errors* which was heavily dependent on its source, the Latin playwright Plautus, with plays based on English history and the Wars of the Roses (*Henry VI* parts 1, 2 and 3, and *Richard III*), and with the bloodthirsty revenge tragedy *Titus Andronicus*. During the 1590s Shakespeare developed his expertise in comedies, writing plays such as *A Midsummer Night's Dream* and *As You Like It*, and produced further plays on medieval English history including *Henry IV* and *Henry V*.

As the new century begins a new note is detectable. Plays such as *Troilus and Cressida* (1601–2) and *Measure for Measure*, sometimes designated 'problem plays' as they poise between comedy and tragedy, evoke complex responses. These plays offer a chronological and generic bridge between the comic period of the 1590s and Shakespeare's tragedies, including *Othello*, *King Lear*, *Macbeth*, *Coriolanus* and *Antony and Cleopatra*, all written in the first decade of the seventeenth century. In the last years of his dramatic career, Shakespeare produced a group of plays often called 'romances'. These plays – *The Tempest*, *Cymbeline* and *The Winter's Tale* reprise many of the situations and themes of the earlier dramas but in fantastical and exotic dramatic designs which, set in distant lands, covering large tracts of time and involving music, mime, dance and tableaux, have something of the qualities of masques and pageants.

THE TEXTS OF SHAKESPEARE'S PLAYS

None of Shakespeare's plays exists in the author's manuscript. Nineteen were printed (not *Measure for Measure*) during his lifetime in small, cheap books called quartos. Shakespeare, however, did not supervise the publication of these plays. This was not unusual. When a playwright had sold a play to a dramatic company he sold his rights in it: copyright, in as much as it existed at this time, belonged to whoever had possession of an actual copy of the text, and so consequently authors had no control over what happened to their work. Several of the quartos do not even mention Shakespeare's name on their title-pages. Unlike the case of a modern author who would prepare his or her work carefully for publication and would receive proof-copies to check for printing errors before the work was circulated, Elizabethan and Jacobean dramatic texts found their way into print in various non-authorial ways. Sometimes an actor's copy of the script, or a prompt copy, perhaps cut or altered for performance, was the basis of the printed text; other quartos seem to derive from an actor or audience member's memory of the play. Printers introduced their own errors, through misreading or making their own 'corrections' where they considered it necessary. Some play-texts, for example the earliest publication of Shakespeare's *Richard II*, also show the marks of censorship.

In 1623, eight years after Shakespeare's death, John Heminges and Henry Condell, two of his fellow actors, collected together texts of thirty-six of his plays (*Pericles* was omitted) and published them together in a large book known as the First **Folio**. There were later editions in 1632, 1663 and 1685. Heminges and Condell promised their readers that these were the texts as Shakespeare had intended them, but this may have been a marketing ploy rather like those modern films which are remarketed as 'the director's cut' despite being essentially the same product as was already available. Despite its appearance and their assurances of its authority, however, the texts in the First Folio still present many difficulties, for there are printing errors and confused passages in the plays, and its texts often differ significantly from those of the earlier quartos, when these exist.

In the case of the text of *Measure for Measure*, the play was first published in the First Folio. There are a number of passages and phrases which have been the subject of intense labour by bibliographers, textual critics and editors. Most modern editions give an abbreviated account of the Folio text (sometimes denoted simply as F) alongside their modernised and emended version, either as a section of collation between the text and the explanatory notes (as in the Arden and World's Classics editions) or as an appendix (as in the Penguin edition). So, for example, the Penguin editor J.M. Nosworthy list over eighty alterations he has made to the Folio text, such as the substitution of 'metal' for the Folio's 'mettle (I.1.48), the insertion of the word 'back' in the Folio's phrase 'call it again' (II.1.58), and the emendation of the Folio's troublesome word 'prenzie' in one instance to 'precise' and in another to 'precious' (III.1.97, 100). The edition also includes numerous additional stage directions, which are often very sparse in early texts.

Shakespeare's texts have, then, been through a number of intermediaries, both in his period and in our own. We do not have his authority for any one of his plays, and hence we cannot know exactly what it was that he wrote. Bibliographers, textual critics and editors have spent a great deal of effort on endeavouring to get behind the apparent errors, uncertainties and contradictions in the available texts to recover the plays as Shakespeare originally wrote them. What we read is the result of these efforts. Modern texts are what editors have constructed from the available evidence: they correspond to no sixteenth- or seventeenth-century editions, and to no early performance of a Shakespeare play. Furthermore, these composite texts differ from each other, for different editors read the early texts differently, perceive different problems and then come to different conclusions. A Shakespeare text is an unstable and a contrived thing.

Often, of course, its judgements embody, if not the personal prejudices of the editor, then the cultural preferences of the time in which he or she was working, Growing awareness of this has led recent scholars to distrust the whole editorial enterprise, and to repudiate the attempt to construct a 'perfect' text. Stanley Wells and Gary Taylor, the editors of the Oxford edition of *The Complete Works* (1986), point out that almost certainly the texts of Shakespeare's plays were altered in performance, and from one performance to another, so that there may never have been a single version. They note, too, that Shakespeare probably revised and rewrote some plays. They do not claim to print a definitive text of any play, but prefer what seems to them the 'more theatrical' version, and when there is a great difference between available versions, as with *King Lear*, they print two texts.

SHAKESPEARE & THE ENGLISH RENAISSANCE

Shakespeare arrived in London at the very time that the Elizabethan period was poised to become the 'golden age' of English Literature. Although Elizabeth reigned as queen from 1558 to 1603, the term 'Elizabethan' is used very loosely in a literary sense to refer to the period 1580 to 1625 when the great works of the age were produced. (Sometimes the later part of this period is distinguished as 'Jacobean', from the Latin form of the name of Elizabeth's successor, James VI of Scotland and I of England, who reigned from 1603 to 1625.) The poet Edmund Spenser heralded this new literary age with his **pastoral** poem *The Shepheardes Calender* (1579), and in his essay *An Apologie for Poetrie*

SHAKESPEARE & THE ENGLISH RENAISSANCE   BACKGROUND

(written in about 1580 and published in 1595), his patron Sir Philip Sidney championed the imaginative power of the 'speaking picture of poetry', famously declaring that 'Nature never set forth the earth in so rich a tapestry as divers poets have done ... Her world is brazen, the poets only deliver a golden'.

Spenser and Sidney were part of that rejuvenating movement in European culture which since the nineteenth century has been known by the term *Renaissance*. Meaning literally 'rebirth' it denotes a revival and redirection of artistic and intellectual endeavour which began in Italy in the fourteenth century and reached England in the early sixteenth century. Its keynote was a curiosity in thought which challenged the old assumptions and traditions: as the poet John Donne was to put it in 'An Anatomy of the World' published in 1633, 'new Philosophy calls all in doubt'. To the innovative spirit of the Renaissance, the preceding ages appeared dully unoriginal and conformist.

That spirit was fuelled by the rediscovery of many classical texts and the culture of ancient Greece and Rome. This fostered a confidence in human reason and in human potential which, in every sphere, challenged old convictions. The discovery of America and its peoples (Columbus had sailed in 1492) demonstrated that the world was a larger and stranger place than had been thought. The cosmological speculation of Copernicus (later confirmed by Galileo) that the sun, not the earth, was the centre of the planetary system challenged the centuries-old belief that the earth and human beings were at the centre of the universe. The pragmatic political philosophy of Machiavelli seemed to cut politics free from its traditional link with morality, by advising statesmen to use any means to secure a desired end. And the religious movements we know collectively as the Reformation broke with the Roman Catholic church and set the individual conscience, not ecclesiastical authority, at the centre of religious life. Nothing, it seemed, was beyond questioning, nothing impossible, although the fate of the hero of Marlowe's play *Dr Faustus* showed the limits and dangers of such radical freedom. The term 'Renaissance' suggests that this age defined itself in relation to the past. Some historians and literary scholars have preferred to use a term which stresses the period's relationship to the future: 'early modern'. Whereas the idea of the Renaissance focuses intellectual and artistic developments, the early modern period stresses those features of life

more familiar to us now: changing ideas of society, of family, of
sexuality and the roles of men and women, the operations of class or
rank, urban life, economics and questions of personal and cultural
identity.

In its innovative and challenging stance, Shakespeare's drama is a
product of its age, as well as of its creator. It interrogates (examines and
asks questions of) the beliefs, assumptions and politics upon which
Elizabethan society was founded. And although the plays often conclude
in a restoration of order and stability, many critics are inclined to argue
that their imaginative energy goes into subverting, rather than
reinforcing, traditional values. *Measure for Measure* is a key illustration of
Shakespearean drama's preference for active questions rather than
unthinking compliance, with the authority of the play delegated to the
individual members of the audience rather than centralised in a dogmatic
author.

Shakespeare's theatre

The theatre for which Shakespeare wrote his plays was a distinctly
Elizabethan invention. There had been no theatres or acting companies
during the medieval period, when plays – usually on religious subjects –
were performed by travelling groups of players in market-places, inn
yards, and in the halls of great houses. Such actors were regarded by the
authorities as little better than vagabonds and layabouts.

In the late sixteenth century, circumstances coincided to transform
this situation. One influence was intellectual. A number of young men
who had been to the universities of Oxford and Cambridge came to
London in the 1580s and began to write plays based on their knowledge
of classical dramas of ancient Greece and Rome. John Lyly, Christopher
Marlowe and Thomas Kyd wrote full-length plays on secular subjects,
offering a range of characterisation and situation hitherto unattempted in
English drama. Lyly wrote in **prose**, but the other playwrights composed
in the unrhymed **iambic** pentameters (**blank verse**) which the Earl of
Surrey had introduced into English earlier in the sixteenth century. This
was a freer and more expressively medium than the rhymed verse of
medieval drama.

THE GLOBE THEATRE,

On the   Bankside.

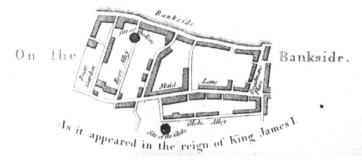

As it appeared in the reign of King James I.

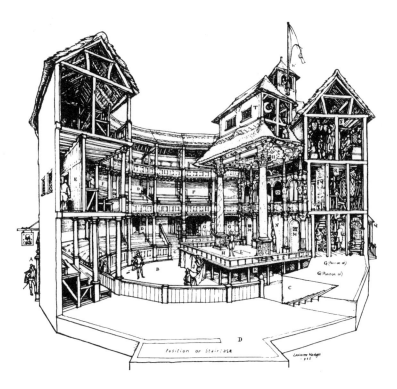

A CONJECTURAL RECONSTRUCTION OF THE INTERIOR OF THE GLOBE PLAYHOUSE

AA Main entrance
B   The Yard
CC Entrances to lowest galleries
D   Entrance to staircase and upper galleries
E   Corridor serving the different sections of the middle gallery
F   Middle gallery ('Twopenny Rooms')
G   'Gentlemen's Rooms or Lords Rooms'
H   The stage
J   The hanging being put up round the stage
K   The 'Hell' under the stage
L   The stage trap, leading down to the Hell
MM Stage doors

N   Curtained 'place behind the stage'
O   Gallery above the stage, used as required sometimes by musicians, sometimes by spectators, and often as part of the play
P   Back-stage area (the tiring-house)
Q   Tiring-house door
R   Dressing-rooms
S   Wardrobe and storage
T   The hut housing the machine for lowering enthroned gods, etc., to the stage
U   The 'Heavens'
W   Hoisting the playhouse flag

Another influence on the establishment of a professional theatre was a new law forbidding travelling players unless they were under the patronage of a nobleman. (Shakespeare's company was under the patronage of the Lord Chamberlain.) This ensured that only the best troupes survived, and that their activity centred on London, where their patrons attended the queen at court. In 1576 the entrepreneur James Burbage built the first permanent playhouse, called 'The Theatre', in Shoreditch just beyond London's northern boundary. Other theatre buildings followed, mostly just outside the city walls or on the south bank of the river Thames to avoid the regulations of London's civic authorities. The theatre was not the middle-class, respectable institution of modern times: it was associated with prostitution, pickpocketing and with the spread of plague. It was blamed for encouraging idleness and criminality, and some extreme preachers argued that the whole system of acting was a form of lying and therefore of sin. Local residents complained about the numbers of people who congregated at the theatre, and, when carriages became popular in the Jacobean period, the congestion on London Bridge caused by playgoers prompted the first parking regulations.

Shakespeare's company performed at Burbage's Theatre until 1596, and also used the Swan and Curtain theatres until moving into their own new building, the Globe, in 1599. It was burned down in 1613 when the thatched roof was ignited by a spark from a cannon fired during a performance of Shakespeare's *Henry VIII*. The Globe theatre has recently been reconstructed, using the available evidence, on Bankside, which offers some sense of the experience of theatregoing for Shakespeare's audiences.

The form of the Elizabethan theatre derived from the inn-yards and animal baiting rings which provided other kinds of entertainment. They were circular wooden buildings with a paved courtyard in the middle open to the sky. A rectangular stage jutted out into the yard, or pit, where some audience members paid a penny to stand and watch the play. Round the perimeter of the yard were tiered galleries, covered with thatch, providing more expensive seats for wealthier spectators. Performances took place in the afternoons to make use of daylight. The yard was about 80ft (24m.) in diameter, and the stage measured about 40ft (12m.) by 30ft (9m.) at 5ft (1.67m.) high, and the theatre could hold about 3,000 spectators. The stage itself was partially covered by a roof or canopy which projected from the wall at the rear of the stage and was supported by two posts at the front. Two doors at the back of the stage led into the dressing room (or 'tiring house') and it was by means of these doors that actors entered and left the stage. Between the doors was a small recess or alcove which was curtained off to provide a 'discovery space', and over the discovery space was a balcony. In the early years of the seventeenth century, Shakespeare's company acquired a smaller indoor theatre called Blackfriars which could seat about 700 people. As a more expensive venue, this theatre probably catered to an audience of a higher social rank. Blackfriars had facilities for more elaborate stage effects, including a machine for lowering actors from above the stage, and these new possibilities were incorporated in Shakespeare's late plays.

There was little in the way of large-scale scenery, which is why Shakespeare's characters often tell us at great length where they are or what their surroundings are like or that it is dark or dawn or stormy. As locations were not represented visually, they have more power as **symbolic** places, perhaps suggesting an inner landscape or psychological state rather than a specific geographical place. Props and costumes were probably also limited. All the roles, including women, were played by male actors. These factors, together with the form of the playhouse, meant that audiences were always aware that they were watching a play. The drama of the period often draws explicit attention to itself *as* drama, using non-naturalistic conventions such as **soliloquy**, the imagery of theatrical performance, or by exploring issues of disguise, role-playing, and the gap between appearance and reality.

The early modern theatre was not concerned to make its audience believe what it was watching was really happening – the recognition of the artificiality of the spectacle was key to the theatrical experience. Modern theatres, by contrast, use lighting and conventions of audience behaviour to encourage spectators to forget themselves as they become absorbed by the action on stage. The auditorium is usually dark, with a passive, silent, and attentive audience watching a spotlight stage where actors are vocal, demonstrative and dramatic. By all accounts, Shakespeare's theatre was quite different. Audience members went to be seen as much as to see, they were lit by natural light like the actors and wore the same kind of clothing. They had none of our modern deference, arriving late, talking and heckling during the performance, eating, drinking and conducting business. It was all much more like our experience of pantomime, where the artificiality of its conventions are enjoyed, expected and understood. But calling a theatre 'the Globe' suggests that it is a microcosm of the world, and the theatre did provide Elizabethan culture with a **metaphor** for understanding its own existence, as in Shakespeare's own famous observation 'All the world's a stage ...' (*As You Like It*).

PART SIX

C RITICAL HISTORY AND BROADER PERSPECTIVES

The most user-friendly selection of critical responses to the play from earliest times to the 1960s will be found in Kenneth Muir's *Casebook* (1968). Bill Overton's *The Winter's Tale* (1989) is a helpful guide to more recent critical approaches; it includes a readable survey of **Marxist, Psychoanalytic** and **feminist** approaches. For undergraduates, Christopher Hardman's volume in the Penguin Critical Studies series (1988) is a model of unpretentious clarity (see Further Reading).

SEVENTEENTH-CENTURY CRITICISM

The earliest mention of *The Winter's Tale* is by Simon Forman, astrologer, quack and sometime physician to Elizabeth I. He saw the play performed at the Globe Theatre, probably very shortly after it was written, in 1611. For him, the play offered a timely warning against the likes of Autolycus: 'Beware of trusting feined beggars or fawninge fellouss'. Forman is an unreliable reporter but some critics have argued that his failure to mention the spectacular statue scene, (an episode not found in *Pandosto*) may be because Shakespeare revised *The Winter's Tale* in the light of theatrical experience.

With or without the statue scene, the play was immediately popular, despite Ben Jonson's jibes (1631) about Shakespeare's offences against common sense and his imaginative geography (Bohemia is a landlocked country). The play was performed a number of times at the Globe, probably also at the indoor theatre at Blackfriars and at Court. We know it was revived in 1613 as part of the celebrations of Princess Elizabeth's wedding. But after its 1633 performance to Charles I, the play fell out of favour for a century and its particular strengths, the synthesizing of **comedy** and **tragedy**, its 'failure' to observe the **unities** of time, action and place, and its rejection of **realism** proved to be what most revolted classically tempered **Augustan critics**. Dryden (1672) dismissed the play as 'grounded in impossibilities', found the comedy unappealing, the tragedy impossible to take seriously.

EIGHTEENTH-CENTURY CRITICISM

Pope (1725) doubted Shakespeare to have written the major part of *The Winter's Tale* whilst Charlotte Lennox (1753) sounds the characteristic **Augustan** note: 'How ridiculous also in a great Queen ... to submit to such buffoonery as standing on a pedestal'. When *The Winter's Tale* was revived in London in the early 1740s it was the **pastoral** scenes which were most admired. It is a truism in the history of Shakespearean criticism that plays which fail to satisfy scholars often triumph in the theatre. However, eighteenth-century performances of Shakespeare invariably presented him in versions 'bottled' to suit prevailing tastes. The most successful rewrite by Garrick, *Florizel and Perdita* (1756), set the action entirely in Bohemia.

NINETEENTH-CENTURY CRITICISM

Shakespeare's version resurfaced in 1811 and Hazlitt (1817) pronounced it 'one of the best-acting of our author's plays'. He was fulsome in his praise of 'Shakespeare's peculiar manner of conveying the painful struggle of different thoughts and feelings, labouring for utterance, and almost strangled in the birth' in Leontes's **soliloquies**. Coleridge (1818) offered all students of *The Winter's Tale* some useful advice; 'it should be immediately followed by the perusal of *Othello* (1604), which is the direct contrast of it in every particular'. Eighty years later, Bernard Shaw put the case more robustly: 'Leontes is a magnificent part, worth fifty Othellos (Shakespeare knew nothing about jealousy when he wrote *Othello*), as modern as Ibsen, and full of wonderful music'.

    Their fairy-tale elements made *The Winter's Tale* and *Cymbeline* (1609) popular with Victorian audiences, productions becoming increasingly elaborate in their use of scenery, rich costume and spectacular lighting effects. Students will find a handy study of some of the ways the apparently impossible statue scene was managed in the introduction to Stephen Orgel's Oxford edition (*The Winter's Tale: The Oxford Shakespeare*, 1996). For Thomas Campbell (1834): 'this statue-scene has hardly its parallel for enchantment even in Shakespeare's theatre. The star of his genius was at its zenith when he composed it' (*Life of Mrs Siddons*, see Muir, ed., *The Winter's Tale: A Casebook*, Macmillan, 1968). However, the Victorians' desire for the most elaborate presentation of every scene meant that Shakespeare's text was usually severely cut.

Also very much to Victorian taste was Shakespeare's presentation of three very different, equally admirable women: Hermione, Paulina and Perdita. Anna Jameson's book, *Shakespeare's Heroines* (1833) offers a fascinating foil to recent **feminist** readings of these characters.

EARLY-TWENTIETH-CENTURY CRITICISM

It was not until Harley Granville Barker's (1912) radical reappraisal at the beginning of the twentieth century of how Shakespeare might have worked on an Elizabethan stage that the play was finally restored in the theatre to something approaching its original form.

Critical studies of the play since Barker's time have had a great deal to say about the problematic, or otherwise, nature of the play's structure and genre. As one of the group now generally thought of as Shakespeare's late plays (*Pericles* – 1608, *The Winter's Tale* – 1610, *Cymbeline* – 1609, *The Tempest* – 1611 and *Henry VIII* – 1613) its status has risen and fallen according to the popularity of that group as a whole. Where Dowden (1875) saw them as the product of their author's terminal tranquillity, H.B. Charlton and Lytton Strachey (1922) regarded the late plays as evidence of Shakespeare's encroaching senility, products of a period when he turned away from the 'real' world of the great tragedies, bored with everything but poetry, the old man at Stratford grown sentimental in his dotage. Others were excited by their common interest in the theme of reconciliation and the playwright's evident faith in the future. There is now widespread agreement that this group of plays reflects a particular stage of Shakespeare's own development: as a poet, as a dramatist and as a thinker. E.M.W. Tillyard's *Shakespeare Last Plays* (1938) is an accessible rebuff to the disparaging arguments of Strachey and although it lacks minute attention to textual detail, the book attempts to show how *The Winter's Tale* represents a progression, a development of Shakespeare's interests in the great tragedies rather than a doddering relapse.

The interest excited by T.S. Eliot's poem *The Waste Land* (1922) and, subsequently, with the anthropological works which exerted a powerful influence on its composition, led many mid-century critics to explore the **symbolic** and mythical elements in Shakespeare's late plays and, at times, to lose sight of their intimate relationship with Shakespeare's mature **tragedies** and **comedies**. Anyone interested in such an approach can find in Jessie Weston's *From Ritual to Romance* (Doubleday, 1920), a study of how primitive vegetation myths developed into the Arthurian legends (it is the book Eliot claimed had shaped *The Waste Land*), many tantalising pre-echoes of this story about a sick king whose sins make his land barren until it is restored to fertility by the combined efforts of courageous virginal virtue (Perdita and Florizel) and the priest-cum-questor role played by Paulina and Camillo.

The most influential critic to pursue this kind of reading was Northrop Frye. In *The Argument of Comedy* (New York, 1949) and *The Anatomy of Criticism* (Princeton, 1957), he argued that the nature myth of Demeter and Proserpine was what lay behind the apparent death and revival of Hermione. This is no more than Perdita herself suggests. The problem with Frye (and with the numerous small fry thrashing in his wake) is that in discovering the common reservoir of feeling and expression from which the whole of Western Culture draws its sustenance, what is lost sight of is Shakespeare's lightness of touch in using such archetypal material. As Christopher Hardman (1988) puts it: 'this kind of criticism … tends to lead one further and further from the play. The deeper some critics delve beneath the surface, the more anything can be made to seem like anything else'. S.L. Bethell's *The Winter's Tale: A Study* (London, 1947) and his subsequent Clarendon edition of the play (Oxford, 1956) offer in a consolidated, thoroughly thought out reading, a radical interpretation of *The Winter's Tale*. He has no doubt that 'Shakespeare wrote from the standpoint of orthodox Christianity' and 'that it is not too much to claim that the play represents an important moment in the history of Christian civilisation'.

In his *Approach to Shakespeare* (1954 and 1965), Derek Traversi develops a religious reading of the play independent of any particular dogma. Although his reading is often laborious, it focuses tightly on the text, avoiding sweeping generalisations.

As an antidote to such tendencies towards more and more abstract readings of the play, the iconoclastic F.R. Leavis in *The Criticism of Shakespeare's Last Plays* (in *The Common Pursuit*, 1952) found in *The Winter's Tale*, 'the supreme instance of Shakespeare's poetic complexity – of the impossibility ... of considering character, episode, theme, and plot in abstraction from the local effects ... The relations between character, speech and the main themes ... are not such as to invite a psychologising approach'.

Muir makes the point that in the late plays we are forced to watch things through the eyes of the parents rather than as in the earlier comedies and tragedies through the eyes of the children. His *Shakespeare's Comic Sequence* (1979) offers a straightforward reading of the play, drawing attention to the powerful dramatic effect of juxtaposing Leontes's tortured sexual jealousy with the idealised picture of sexless childhood innocence painted in Polixenes's speech (I.2.67–75) without commenting on their equal morbidity. Muir claims that Paulina is 'lying' (III.2.196–204), imposing a naturalistic, psychological reading upon material better understood in terms of pragmatic theatricality but then corrects himself, 'I think there can be no doubt that even if Shakespeare did not intend Hermione to be dead at this point in the play, he intended us to think so'. It is difficult to see how what Shakespeare 'intended' as a dramatist can be different from what he 'intends' in his development of plot and character. Muir observes shrewdly that objections to the statue scene are made more often by critics in their studies than by people in the audience. He quotes a lively account of Mrs Siddons's performance, 'The heart of everyone who saw her when she burst from the semblance of sculpture into motion ... must throb and glow at the recollection' and an even more exciting one of the production by Macready: '[his] joy at finding Hermione alive seemed uncontrollable ... the audience were tumultuously applauding, with a sound like a storm of hail'.

Two refreshingly accessible and unpretentious readings of the play will be found in D.J. Enright's *Shakespeare and the Critics* (1970) and Wilbur Sanders's volume on the play in the *Harvester New Critical Introductions* series (1987). If Enright is sometimes boorish where Sanders teases subtleties with more wit and nicer discrimination, both books have moments of passionate subjectivity, a welcome antidote to solemn and doctrinaire readings of the play which substitute evangelical agendas of various kinds for sensitive textual analysis and imaginative engagement.

CONTEMPORARY APPROACHES

SHAKESPEARE AND IDEOLOGY

Over the last twenty years, new and radical critical theories have emerged. They ask us to reconsider the way people read any literary text, *The Winter's Tale* included. This does not mean that students must ditch lines of enquiry that have proved interesting and fruitful in the past. But awareness of very different ways of thinking about texts is not only prudent but stimulating. Like any radical departure, what is valuable in modern critical theory will in time become integrated with the approaches of earlier generations, helping us to see more clearly what any single type of critical analysis can and cannot achieve.

Traditional theories see *The Winter's Tale* as a work of art that must be taken as it stands, much of the critic's job being to explore how apparently discordant elements within the play relate to one another in a meaningful way and persuasive way which engages with perennial human concerns. To see the work as showing us something important about human life and human responsibilities.

A feature of much Shakespearean criticism in the second half of the twentieth century is its ideological bias and intensely cerebral nature. It is a by-product of the expansion of English Literature as an academic discipline and the desire by some to prove English as 'rigorous' a subject as Physics. For the student still developing a sound working knowledge of the text, such approaches can be baffling, misleading and demoralizing. Often they present as impersonal fact readings which are as tendentious, subjective and reductivist as anything to be found in the amateur critics of the nineteenth century. Various schools explore Shakespeare's plays from standpoints predetermined by theories about society, culture, language and psychology. The close scrutiny of particular texts and of particular words, images and gestures in texts which distinguished the work of the so-called New Critics of the 1930s (and informs the expectations of most examiners) gives way to generalizations not only about Shakespeare's art as a whole but about Renaissance thought and the processes of early modern culture. Such theories are difficult for students to assimilate, harder still to engage with and challenge, resting as they do upon intellectually demanding theory and a range of reading unlikely to be encompassed by the typical undergraduate. Becoming aware of the direction in which certain kinds of criticism is moving, therefore, needs to proceed with caution if enjoyment of Shakespeare's language, action and the imaginative and dramatic force of his work is not to be traded for a handful of pretentious clichés.

CRITICAL THEORY

What distinguishes radical late-twentieth-century thinkers about the play from those of earlier generations is, above all, their rejection of the idea that any work or any author can achieve the kind of universality which generations of critics have claimed for The Winter's Tale in particular and for Shakespeare more generally – such an idea was crystallized by Ben Jonson in his tribute to Shakespeare that 'He was not of an age, but for all time'. What such critics assert is that any work of art mirrors the beliefs, assumptions, prejudices and blindspots of the society in which it is produced. That no individual can be said to transcend the circumstances in which s/he operates and that any reading is similarly, decisively shaped by the intellectual climate in which it takes place.

STRUCTURALISM

Structuralist critics approach The Winter's Tale as they would any other statement, as an interesting linguistic phenomenon. Rather than search the play in the hope of finding that it tells something about the world or human nature or the relationship of humanity to Eternity, structuralists explore the ways in which key words generate about them force fields of associations and value systems and thus mean more than is immediately apparent. Or mean something rather different from what they may appear to mean to the untrained observer.

POST-STRUCTURALISM

Taking this scepticism a stage further, **post-structuralists** insist upon the ambiguity of any statement or work of art. This differs radically from the belief of critics such as Empson – that great poets use ambiguity on the whole deliberately and in a controlled manner to achieve particular results (see W. Empson, *Seven Types of Ambiguity*, London, 1930). It argues that a work of art has no primary or final meaning. That engaging with *The Winter's Tale*, like engaging with anything else, is more like a perpetual series of chess games in which there will be an almost infinite number of outcomes, none of which is superior to any other, simply different. Post-structuralist criticism revels in the intricate ways language works to generate a rich and bewildering complex of possible meanings.

Other critical approaches which inform a great deal of contemporary thinking about *The Winter's Tale* are less concerned with linguistic studies in a vacuum than with the need to address the political agenda which it is argued any work of literature consciously or unconsciously presents us with. Students will find these and other contemporary critical approaches explored lucidly in Bill Overton's *The Winter's Tale* (1989).

FEMINIST CRITICISM

Feminist criticism, like any other school of criticism, speaks with many different voices. Common to all feminists, however, is the desire to challenge and change assumptions about gender, illuminating the way in which sexual stereotyping is frequently embodied in a text. Literature and the ways in which it has been written about in the past is seen as having contributed to the marginalisation of women and to the denying to women of a voice.

As we have explored in the commentaries, *The Winter's Tale* is remarkable for presenting three very different women as its strongest characters, especially when we remember that all Elizabethan actors were male. Marilyn French (1983) is concerned with the play's exploration of the very ideas of maleness and femaleness. This she explores not only in terms of theme and characterisation but also with reference to the play's dramatic structure, seeing **romance** and the triumph of its conventions as symbolic of a triumph of the feminine though, paradoxically, in doing so, she marginalises the roles of Paulina and Hermione. Lisa Jardine (1983) rejects French's generalised theoretical approach in favour of a study of how 'femaleness' was regarded at the time of the play's first production. Patricia Southgard Gourlay (1975) examines the Renaissance's fascination with Venus and Eve as variously destructive and creative female forces. On the one hand, she sees Leontes's alienation from Hermione as 'symptomatic of his society's alienation from the qualities the women metaphorically represent'. Hermione, Paulina and Perdita, on the other hand represent 'the subversive and creative power of love, art and nature.'

Lisa Jardine, *Still Harping on his Daughters: Women and Drama in the Age of Shakespeare*, Harvester Press, 1983

Patricia Southard Gourlay, '"O my most sacred lady": Female Metaphor in *The Winter's Tale*,' *English Literary Renaissance* 5, 1975

PSYCHOANALYTIC APPROACHES

Despite F.R. Leavis's caveat (see above), many critics have argued that alongside Macbeth and Angelo, Leontes represents one of Shakespeare's most fully psychologically realised protagonists. The debate explores the origins of his jealousy. Is it like a piece of spontaneous combustion or are the seeds of it present at the very beginning of the play?

Some critics have argued that Leontes is struggling with homosexual feelings for Polixenes and that the marriage of Perdita and Florizel represents some kind of sublimation for feelings neither King is able to express.

In the most elaborate case-study, Murray Schwarz (1976) sees the Kings' nostalgia for childhood in **Freudian** terms. It is a myth which 'preserves in masculine form a narcissistic and idealized version of the mother's dual unity with the son' (cited by Overton). As in Ernst Jones's notorious study of *Hamlet* (*Hamlet and Oedipus*, 1949), the emphasis throughout a complex reading is upon unconscious motivation. As Overton comments, 'Too often Schwarz strains the sense in his effort to find evidence'.

Murray M. Schwarz, 'Leontes's Jealousy in *The Winter's Tale*' in
Leonard Tenenhouse, ed., *The Practice of Psychoanalytic Criticism*,
Wayne State University Press, Detroit, 1976

POLITICAL CRITICISM

Where earlier critics determine to find ways to resolve apparent
contradictions and inconsistencies, whether within a single speech or in
the larger design of the play, what the student will often encounter in
Marxist approaches is more like the revelation of fallibility masked by the
illusion of coherence to which not only Shakespeare but those who have
written upon him subsequently have contributed. What is most
consistently challenged is the idea that there can be a 'common-sense'
response to any text which is not as much a product of its author's
historical and cultural situation as was Shakespeare's writing of the play.
The Winter's Tale was produced at a time of unprecedented intellectual
ferment; religious and political controversy in London at the turn of the
seventeenth century pointed towards the Civil War and its resulting new
conceptions of authority within fifty years. The New Historicists call
attention to the fact that this play which dramatises upheavals in two
courts was written at a time when the absolute power of the monarchy
was being tested by the irresistible rise of capitalism. The New
Historicists, unlike the practitioners of the New Criticism, are concerned
less with the words on the page than in the circumstances in which they
were produced. Ideology, the whole value system which informs any
utterance and the reception of any utterance shifts the critical focus from
the particular author and the particular work of art to the complex value
systems in which it came into being. Rather than *The Winter's Tale* being
a powerful creative expression of Shakespeare's understanding of the
universal and timeless human condition, the play is seen as a product of
Elizabethan culture as it passed through a period of extraordinary
upheaval. *The Winter's Tale* dramatises the struggles of its time. As in
feminist so in Marxist criticism it is contended that there can be no
reading of *The Winter's Tale* which is not 'political'.

Charles Barber (1964) for example argues that 'the play is more
directly concerned with the problems of Jacobean society than is usually
recognised' and sees the dramatic contrast and conflict between two

enervated courts presided over by despotic Kings and the compensating humanity of the countryside reconciled in the marriage of Perdita and Florizel as something more than pastoral convention. He sees the play's structure in classic Marxist terms as 'a kind of thesis-antithesis-synthesis pattern'. Bill Overton (1989) develops a more thorough analysis of the significance of the fact that the play's 'two most dangerous characters are kings'. Examining what he calls 'the pathology of monarchy', he argues that the play is concerned with a topical Jacobean theme: the abuse of regal and patriarchal autocratic power. Overton sees Leontes's derangement as less the consequence of jealousy than 'in keeping with possession of unchecked power enjoyed from an early age ... No wonder Leontes is volatile and unstable'. Simon Shepherd (1981) draws parallels between the jealous possessiveness of Polixenes and James I's 'harshness and arbitrariness ... Anything that laid bare James's authoritarian attitudes must have struck home in 1610 because of the debate between king and Parliament over royal prerogative'.

Charles Barber, 'The Winter's Tale and Jacobean Society' in Arnold Kettle, ed., Shakespeare in a Changing World, Lawrence & Wishart, 1964

Simon Shepherd, Amazons and Warrior Women: Varieties of Feminism in Seventeenth-Century Drama, Harvester Press, 1981

SHAKESPEARE IN PERFORMANCE

But for the student still getting to know the play, probably the most accessible interpretations of recent years are the increasing number of performances of The Winter's Tale available on audio and videotape and criticism which concerns itself with the way each performance of a Shakespeare play is an investigation and a reading.

Two books – David Male's Shakespeare on Stage: The Winter's Tale (CUP, 1984) and R.P. Draper's The Winter's Tale: Text and Performance (Macmillan, 1985) – dealing with productions by Trevor Nunn (1969), John Barton (1976) , Jane Howell (1980) and Ronald Eyre (1981), and including photographs taken from them, are useful for their discussion of the practical as distinct from the metaphysical problems and rewards the play presents. Andrew Gurr's The Shakespearean Stage 1574–1642

(Cambridge, revised 1980) explores the conditions in which *The Winter's Tale* first became familiar to audiences whilst D. Bartholomeusz's *The Winter's Tale in Performance in England and America, 1611–1976* (Cambridge, 1982) discusses its subsequent stage history.

FURTHER READING

John Dryden, Defence of the Epilogue to the Second Part of *The Conquest of Granada*, 1672

Alexander Pope, *Preface to his edition of Shakespeare*, 1725

William Hazlitt, *Characters of Shakespeare's Plays*, 1817

Edward Dowden, *Shakespeare – His Mind and Art*, 1875

Harley Granville-Barker, *Prefaces to Shakespeare, Volume VI*, Batsford, London, 1974

> Reprints the essay of 1912 written in the light of Granville-Barker's restoration of the play in its original form on stage. Robust and unpretentious

Jessie L Weston, *From Ritual to Romance*, Doubleday Anchor, New York, 1920

> The book which influenced Eliot's The Wasteland explores the development of ancient fertility rituals into Arthurian **romance**. Indirectly, it offers advanced students some fruitful and provocative ways of reading Shakespeare's late plays

E.M.W. Tillyard, *Shakespeare's Last Plays*, Chatto, London, 1938

> A readable book written in response to the dismissive views of Strachey. Tillyard argues that the late plays represent a culmination of Shakespeare's dramatic development

F.R. Leavis, *The Common Pursuit*, Chatto, London, 1952

> Includes a characteristically robust, stimulating and provocative response to those who would attempt to psychoanalyse characters in Shakespeare's late plays

Derek Traversi, *Shakespeare: The Last Phase*, Hollis & Carter, London, 1954

> Thorough, stolid but scrupulously attentive to textual detail

S.L. Bethell, ed., *The Winter's Tale*, Oxford, 1956

> For many years, the standard school edition of the play. Includes excellent notes and a forceful introduction, interpreting the play as profoundly Christian

Frank Kermode, ed., *The Winter's Tale*, Signet, New York, 1963
Includes a lively introduction, selections from *Pandosto* and extracts from several major critical essays

J.H.P. Pafford, ed., *The Winter's Tale*, Arden, Routledge, 1963
Includes an extensive introduction, a sometimes bewildering amount of textual annotation and the full text of *Pandosto*

Kenneth Muir, ed., *The Winter's Tale: A Casebook*, Macmillian, 1968
An invaluable anthology of critical responses to the play from Forman to Mahood

Ernest Schanzer, ed., *The Winter's Tale*, Penguin, 1969
The edition on which these notes have been based. Includes a searching introductory essay and a helpful commentary

Lisa Jardine, *Still Harping on Daughters, Women and Drama in the Age of Shakespeare*, Harvester Wheatsheaf, 1983
An important book in the development of **feminist** readings of Shakespeare

R.P. Draper, *The Winter's Tale, Text and Performance*, Macmillan, London, 1985
Includes useful accounts (and some photographs) of four important productions of the play, 1969–1980

Wilbur Sanders, *The Winter's Tale*, Harvester Press, 1987
For the undergraduate, the most poised, witty and searching reading of the play of recent years

Christopher Hardman, *The Winter's Tale*, Penguin, 1988
For advanced students who know the text, a well-informed and lucid guide to the play and some of its problems

Bill Overton, *The Winter's Tale*, Macmillan, 1989
For undergraduates, a thorough and readable survey of recent critical approaches to *The Winter's Tale* followed by a stimulating appraisal of ways modern audiences might engage with the play and the issues it raises

Stephen Orgel, ed., *The Winter's Tale*, OUP, 1996
For undergraduates, the standard, scholarly edition of the text. It includes an extensive introduction, detailed textual annotation and the full text of *Pandosto*

Events in Europe	Shakespeare's life	Literary events
1559 Coronation of Elizabeth I		
	1564 Born in Stratford-upon-Avon	
1577 Francis Drake leaves Plymouth aboard *Pelican* to sail round the world, returning in 1580		
1582 Outbreak of the Plague in London	**1582** Marries Anne Hathaway	
	1583 His daughter, Susanna, is born	
	1585 His twins, Hamnet and Judith, are born	
1587 Mary Queen of Scots is executed		**1587** Christopher Marlowe, *Tamburlaine the Great*
		1588 Robert Greene's novel *Pandosto, or the Triumph of Time* published
		1590 Edmund Spenser, *The Faerie Queen*
1592 Plague in London leads to the closing of theatres until 1594	**1592** *The Comedy of Errors*	**1592** Christopher Marlowe, *Doctor Faustus*
	1593 *Richard III*, *The Two Gentlemen of Verona* and *Titus Andronicus*	**1593** Christopher Marlowe is killed in tavern brawl at Deptford
	1594 *The Taming of the Shrew*	
	1595 *Loves Labours Lost, Romeo and Juliet*, and *A Midsummer Night's Dream*	**1595** Jean Florio's translations of Montaigne's, *Essaies* published
	1596 Hamnet dies. *The Merchant of Venice*	

Events in Europe	Shakespeare's life	Literary events
	1597 *Henry IV parts I* and *II;* Shakespeare purchases New Place, Stratford-upon-Avon	
1598 Death of King Phillip II of Spain	**1598** *Much Ado About Nothing*	**1598** Ben Jonson, *Every Man in his Humour*
	1599 Globe Theatre opens in London; *Julius Caesar, Henry V* and *As You Like It*	
	1600 *The Merry Wives of Windsor* and *Twelfth Night*	
1601 Poor Law Act passed by Parliament	**1601** *Hamlet,* John Shakespeare (father) dies	**1601** John Marston, *What You Will*
	1602 *Troilus and Cressida* and *All's Well That Ends Well*	
1603 Death of Elizabeth I, and accession of James I	**1603** Shakespeare's company is granted a royal patent by James I and becomes 'The King's Men'	
1604 Hampton Court Conference agrees a new 'authorised' translation of the Bible is needed	**1604** *Othello* and *Measure for Measure*	
1605 The Gunpowder plot – Guy Fawkes is arrested while preparing explosives in the cellar of the Palace of Westminster	**1605** *King Lear*	**1605** Miguel de Cervantes Saavedra, Spanish novelist, *Don Quixote*
1606 James I proclaims a national flag ('Union Jack') that combines the St George's cross and St Andrews saltire	**1606** *Macbeth* and *Antony and Cleopatra*	**1606** Ben Jonson, *Volpone*
	1607 *Timon of Athens*	

Events in Europe	Shakespeare's life	Literary events
	1608 *Coriolanus* and *Pericles;* Mary Shakespeare (mother) dies	
	1609 *Sonnets* published	
	1609-10 Probable date for the composition of *The Winter's Tale*	
	1610-11 Probable date for the composition of *Cymbeline*	
1611 Authorised Version of the Bible is published	1611 *The Tempest;* Simon Forman sees *The Winter's Tale* and *Cymbeline* at the Globe Theatre; *The Winter's Tale* performed at Court before James I	1611 Ben Jonson's masque *Oberon* performed at Court
1612 King James's popular son Henry, Prince of Wales, dies		
	1613 Globe Theatre burns down; reopens 1614; *The Winter's Tale* performed at Court as part of Princess Elizabeth's betrothal celebrations	
		1614 John Webster, *The Duchess of Malfi*
	1616 William Shakespeare dies	1616 Inigo Jones designs the Queen's House, Greenwich; folio of Ben Jonson's *Works* published
1620 A group of settlers, later to be called the Pilgrim Fathers, set sail in the *Mayflower* for the New World		
	1623 *The Winter's Tale* is printed as the last of Shakespeare's Comedies in the First Folio	
1625 James I dies, and is succeeded by Charles I		

Augustan critics Addison, Steele, Pope and swift all admired the Roman writers of the Augustan age and attempted to imitate them in style and subject matter

blank verse unrhymed iambic pentameter

chorus in the tragedies of the ancient Greek playwrights Aeschylus and Sophocles, the Chorus is a group of characters who represent ordinary people who comment upon the action which they witness as bystanders. In Shakespeare's plays, however, the Chorus acts as a narrator, giving the audience information there is not stage-time enough to dramatise. Shakespeare often uses a character not otherwise engaged to act as a temporary Chorus/Narrator to help things flow smoothly

classical unities see unities

colloquial/colloquialism the use of the kinds of expression and grammar associated with ordinary, everyday speech than rather formal language

comedy (Gk. 'merry-making, comic poet') a broad genre which encompasses a large variety of different kinds of literature; however, 'comedy' is used most often with reference to a kind of drama which is intended primarily to entertain the audience, and which ends happily for the characters.

In this meaning of the word, 'comedy', like tragedy, is an ancient form dating at least as far back as the fifth century BC. It probably originated in the seasonal festivities, often obscene, which were part of the Dionysiac fertility cult. By the end of the fifth century BC great individual playwrights had already emerged: Aristophanes is the most notable. His plays, such as *The Frogs* and *Lysistrata*, combine lyrical poetry, buffoonery, satire and fantastical plots and characters. Another highly prized writer of comedies was Menander, who flourished at the end of the fourth century BC: his plays are only known because of his strong influence on the Roman playwrights Plautus and Terence. Their comedies are more social in their focus, contain songs, and have elaborate plots, involving stock characters, such as the bragging soldier, spendthrift young men, wily servants, and so on, many of whom were copied by Renaissance playwrights; Shakespeare's *The Comedy Of Errors* (*c.*1592–3), for example, is modelled on the *Menaechmi* of Plautus.

During the Middle Ages the word 'comedy' referred to narrative poetry in which the plot ends happily. Dante's *Divine Comedy* (*c.*1304–21) is perhaps not typical of this usage, though Dante's progress through the 'Inferno' and 'Purgatory' to 'Paradise' shows the basic 'comic' pattern of movement from trouble and misery towards happiness. There were farcical interludes in the medieval mystery plays, but it was during the Renaissance that comic drama flourished once more and developed a wide variety of styles and interests.

Perhaps because Aristotle concentrated on tragedy in the *Poetics* (fourth century BC), comedy was never subject to the same attempt to impose rules concerning its conventions. But none the less most comedies from the Renaissance until the present day share certain features: they do not concentrate on the fortunes of an individual, but the interest is spread over a group of people; they tend to deal with low life and humble people, rather than with kings and nobles; their plots are usually elaborate, involve misunderstandings and deceptions, and move from the possibility of disaster towards a happy ending, often symbolised by a wedding. All these elements distinguish comedy strongly from tragedy (though, of course, the forms are mixed in tragicomedy from the Renaissance onwards).

Different forms of comedy are also clearly discernible. **Romantic comedy**, such as Shakespeare's *As You Like It* (*c*.1599), involves idealised lovers sorting out their tangled relationship and achieving happiness: it is light-hearted and unrealistic. **Satiric comedy** in the manner of Ben Jonson's *Volpone* (1605–6) may be painfully unflinching in its depiction of human folly, vice and greed: it concentrates on the clever unscrupulousness of tricksters and the stupid gullibility of their dupes. **The comedy of manners**, which reaches its point of perfection during the Restoration and the eighteenth century, focuses on the love intrigues of cynical and sophisticated young aristocrats in high society: it relies heavily on verbal wit, while the other comic styles often contain farcical elements or even slapstick. **Farce**, which concentrates wholly on provoking laughter, is quite a late development in drama

coup de théâtre (Fr. 'theatrical blow') a sudden and spectacular turn to events in the plot of a play, such as a surprise revelation or unmasking, that changes the audience's perception of the action

deconstruction most of the ideas of deconstruction originate in the difficult works of the French philosopher, Jacques Derrida. He believes that all notions of the existence of an absolute meaning in language are wrong; yet this assumption has dominated Western thought and it should be the aim of the philosopher and critic, Derrida argues, to 'deconstruct' the philosophy and literature of the past to show this false assumption and reveal the essential paradox at the heart of language. To 'deconstruct' a text is merely to show how texts deconstruct themselves because of the fundamental indeterminateness at the core of language. One reason for the difficulty of Derrida's own writing is that he is aware of his own texts deconstructing themselves.

The word 'deconstruction' is now often used merely to refer to the revelation of partially hidden meanings in a text, especially those that illuminate aspects of its relationship with its social and political context. In its weakest form, it has become a jargon word for 'analyse' or 'interpret'

denouement (Fr. 'unknotting') the final unfolding of a plot: the point at which the reader's expectations, be they hopes or fears, about what will happen to the characters are finally satisfied or denied

diction the choice of words in a work of literature – the kind of vocabulary used

dramatic irony something which one is aware of only on a second or third reading of a play. Dramatic irony occurs when words spoken on stage have far more significance than the speaker is aware of. It places the audience (or reader) in a privileged position, detached from the action

feminist criticism since the late 1960s feminist theories about literature and language, and feminist interpretations of texts, have multiplied enormously. A tenet of feminist thought is that male ways of perceiving and ordering are 'inscribed' into the prevailing ideology of society. This can be disclosed by studying language itself, and texts, in order to discover the characteristic assumptions which are inherent in them. In patriarchal societies – also called 'androcentric (Gk. 'man-centred') or 'phallocratic' (Gk. 'penis-ruled') – language contains binary oppositions of qualities such as active/passive, adventurous/timid, or reasonable/irrational, in which, it is argued, the feminine is always associated with the less desirable words in the listed pairs. Women are subordinated because they are perceived through this constantly repeated framework of negative perceptions which are inherent in language. Areas of human achievement are defined in terms of male ideas and aspirations, and the presumption that advances in civilisation have always been brought about by men. Women are thus conditioned to enter society accepting their own inferiority, and even co-operating in and approving its perpetuation. Femininity is regarded as a construct of society

folio (Latin 'leaf') a large page size, formed by a single fold in a sheet of printer's paper, giving four pages (or sides). Shakespeare's plays were first collected by

Heminges and Condell in the volume called the First Folio (1623). Before this only nineteen of his plays had been published, all of them in unauthorised Quarto editions (a quarto page being half the size of the folio page, formed by another fold in the printer's sheet). Bibliographical discussion of Shakespeare's plays refers continually to different Quarto and Folio texts

Freudian see Psychoanalytic criticism

hyperbole (Gk. 'throwing too far') a figure of speech: emphasis by exaggeration. Common in everyday speech: 'There were millions of people at the cafe.' Common also in all kinds of literature, comic and serious

iamb the commonest metrical foot in English verse – consisting of a weak stress followed by a strong stress, e.g. ti-tum

iconography the conventional significance attached to symbols

innuendo an indirect or subtle reference, especially one made maliciously or indicating criticism, disapproval or bawdy

malapropism mistaken and muddled use of long words

Marxist Criticism criticism that considers literature in relation to its capacity to reflect the struggle between the classes and economic conditions

metaphor a figure of speech in which a word or phrase is applied to an object or action that it does not literally denote in order to imply a resemblance

metaphysical poetry verse of the early seventeenth century remarkable for its intellectual rigour and delight in elaborate, extended metaphors

New Criticism a major critical movement that recommended that a poem must be studied as a poem and not as a piece of biographical or sociological evidence, or literary-historical material, or as a demonstration of a psychological theory of literature, or for any other reason. Close reading of texts became the only legitimate critical procedure seeing the work as a linguistic structure

New Historicism the work of critics who discuss literary works in terms of their historical contexts, often minutely researched, as a reaction against New Criticism and Structuralism

ostinato continuously reiterated phrase

pastoral (Latin 'to do with shepherds') the pastoral describes an imaginary world of simple, idealised rural life, in which shepherds and shepherdesses fall in love, enjoying a life of blissful ease, singing songs, playing the flute, and so on. Marlowe's 'The Passionate Shepherd to His Love' (1599) suggests the conscious artificiality of the genre:

And I will make thee beds of Roses,
And a thousand fragrant posies,
A cap of flowers, and a kirtle
Embroidered all with leaves of Myrtle ...
A belt of straw, and Ivy buds,
With Coral clasps and Amber studs,
And if these pleasures may thee move,
Come live with me and be my love.

No one could be mistaken into thinking this concerns the life and habits of real shepherds. Pastorals usually deal with a perfect, mythical world, set far back in time, a Golden Age of uncorrupted rural simplicity, Gods and goddesses and other supernatural beings such as nymphs are its inhabitants.

The genre originates with the *Idylls* of Theocritus, a Greek poet living in Sicily in the third century BC. These narratives about gods and shepherds were the model for the Eclogues (42–37BC) of the Roman poet Virgil which in turn became the model for the pastoral poetry and prose written in Europe during the Renaissance. Shakespeare uses many of the conventions of pastoral in *As You Like It* (c.1599): sophisticated courtiers meet rustic yokels and ardent shepherd boys in the Forest of Arden, where everything eventually ends happily. Spenser's *Shepherd's Calendar* (1579) is another example. Pastoral elements find their way into prose, for instance, Sidney's *The Arcadia* (1590). Indeed *As You Like It* is based on a pastoral romance, mainly in prose, by Thomas Lodge.

The Christian idea of Christ as a shepherd allowed the pastoral to be adapted and to develop other allegorical associations. Its conventions remained valid till the early eighteenth century: Pope's *Pastorals* appeared in 1709. From the mid-eighteenth century onwards poems of country life began to focus more realistically on their subject. Crabbe's *The Village* (1783) declared its aim to depict the labourer's cottage 'As truth will paint it, and as bards will not'. Wordsworth's *Michael* (1800) is subtitled 'A Pastoral Poem', but only ironically: it is a realistic tale about shepherds. However, Wordsworth does hint at the artifice of the pastoral in 'Intimations of Immortality' (1807), asking to 'hear thy shouts, thou happy shepherd-boy!' Aspects of the pastoral continue to crop up in nineteenth- and twentieth-century poetry: the pastoral elegy in particular remained in use as a poetic convention after the artifices of the ordinary pastoral had been withered by the assumptions of realism

pathos moments in works of art which evoke strong feelings of pity and sorrow are said to have this quality

prose any language that is not made patterned by the regularity of some kind of metre

Psychoanalytic criticism Freud developed the theory of psychoanalysis as a means of curing neuroses in his patients, but its concepts were expanded by him and his followers as a means of understanding human behaviour and culture generally. Literature, for Freud, is produced by the same mechanism as dreams. Desires, mainly sexual, in conflict with social norms, are censored and pushed into the subconscious ('represses'), from which they emerge in forms (e.g. non-sexual goals such as writing and painting) that are modified, disguised and all but unrecognisable to the conscious mind. The critic's task is to reveal the true latent content of literature, the psychological realities that underlie the work or art

realism the word has many applications, but broadly speaking it refers to the tendency in literature to portray the real world without softening its appearance (as idealist kinds of writing would tend to do); realism aims to tell the unglossed truth about reality. It refers to a set of conventions by which the real might be expressed rather than to reality itself. Realism was the dominant mode of nineteenth-century fiction, but its application is often misleading to students because of the subjects that realism could not consider in the context of a conservative audience. The reality realism portrayed was often very selective

rhythm the chief element of rhythm is the patterning of stressed and unstressed syllables

romance since the appearance of an essay by Dowden (1877), some critics, looking for a distinct generic term to apply to Shakespeare's late plays (from *Pericles* to *The Tempest*) have used the term 'Romance' in preference to 'Tragicomedy'. Like Coleridge before him, Dowden stressed the significance of 'romantic' features in these plays: children lost and recovered, the use of beautiful rural settings for part of the action and the 'miraculous' nature of some of the action. In the latest Oxford edition of *The Winter's Tale* (1996), Stephen Orgle observes: 'The new genre ... has proved as obfuscatory as it has been enlightening'. Attempts to categorise Shakespeare plays usually reveal more about the mentality of the critic than about the work s/he is discussing.

soliloquy a dramatic convention which allows a character in a play to speak directly to the audience about his/her motives, feelings and decisions as if s/he were thinking aloud. Part of the convention is that a soliloquy reveals a character's innermost thoughts and feelings: we learn more about the character than could ever be gathered from the action of the play

stress in spoken English, some syllables are stressed more than others: in **sp**oken **Eng**lish, **some syll**ables are **stressed more** than **oth**ers

structuralism and post-structuralism structuralism examines aspects of human society, including language, literature and social institutions, as integrated structures or systems in which the parts have no real existence of their own, but derive meaning and significance only from their place within the system. For example, the basic unit of meaning in language, the phoneme (basic sound unit), is seen to derive its meaning not from any inherent qualities in itself, but because of its 'difference' from other sounds. Structuralist critics often explore individual works in literature by analysing them in terms of linguistic concepts, such as the phoneme, or as if the structure of a work resembled the syntax of a sentence. Others concentrate on examining the conventions and expectations which a knowledgeable reader understands implicitly when reading the work, with the ultimate aim of building up a kind of grammar or ground-plan of the whole system of literature and its place in society.

Structuralism has now been superseded by the even more radical post-structuralist theories, also known as deconstruction

symbol (Gk. 'mark, sign, token', originally 'put together') a symbol is something which represents something else (often an idea or quality) by analogy or association. Writers use conventional symbols (white=innocence; lion=courage; rose=beauty and fragility) but also they invent their own

tableau (French 'picture painted on wood') a picture; especially a pictorial grouping of persons in a drama. A *tableau vivant* is a living picture, a silent and motionless group of persons arranged so as to represent a dramatic or melodramatic scene. A set piece describing such a picture – such as a grouping of people in a novel or poem – would also be called a tableau

tragedy (Gk. 'goat song') possibly the most homogenous and easily recognised genre in literature, and certainly one of the most discussed. Basically a tragedy traces the career and downfall of an individual, and shows in this downfall both the capacities and the limitations of human life. The protagonist may be superhuman, a monarch or, in the modern age, an ordinary person. It is possible to imagine a tragic action involving a group of people, but unless they were seen as in some way outside the rest of society, some of the essential quality of tragedy, which seems to include an element of the scapegoat or sacrifice (implicit in the derivation of the word 'tragedy'), would be lost.

Aristotle in his *Poetics* (fourth century BC) began the debate about what made true tragedy, or what factors made it most compelling. He based his observations on the study of the tragedies performed annually at Athens from the sixth century BC onwards. These occasions were partly religious rites and partly competitions for dramatists. Greek tragedy was performed by professional actors who wore masks and high shoes called buskins, and by a chorus of citizens who also danced. The greatest fifth-century BC Greek tragedians whose works are known to us are Aeschylus, Sophocles and Euripides; of the many plays they wrote only a few survive. Aristotle analysed tragedy in his *Poetics*. He observed that it represented a single action of a certain magnitude, that it provoked in the audience the emotions of pity and terror which were then resolved or dissolved by catharsis at the play's climax, and that certain features of the plot were common, notably the existence of some connection between the protagonist's downfall and preceding behaviour (hamartia, 'error') and the process of the 'reversal of fortune' (peripeteia) and the moments of 'discovery' (anagnorisis) by which the protagonist learned the truth of his or her situation. Many of Aristotle's terms and ideas are still accepted as valuable insights into the nature of tragic drama. However, his theory of the unities of time and space and some of his other ideas came to be regarded as prescriptive formulae for the construction of true tragedy, especially in France during the seventeenth century, and in this respect his influence has also been constricting, though the *Poetics* itself does not make claims to be authoritative, and the unities are not a specially significant part of Aristotle's argument.

Seneca was the most influential Roman tragedian: his plays were probably not meant to be performed on stage, though he borrowed his subjects from the Greek playwrights.

In the Middle Ages tragedy was regarded simply as the story of an eminent person who suffers a downfall. The Classical tragedies and theories of Aristotle were unknown.

In English literature the Elizabethan and Jacobean periods are the great age of tragedy. Seneca provided the model both for the formal Classical tragedy with five acts and elaborate style, for example, Sackville and Norton's *Gorboduc* (1561), and for the popular revenge tragedies or tragedies of blood, full of horrific violent incidents and sensational elements, in which a quest for vengeance leads to a bloodthirsty climax. Kyd's *The Spanish Tragedy* (*c*.1589) and Webster's *The Duchess of Malfi* (*c*.1613) and *The White Devil* (*c*.1612) are notable examples of this form. Shakespeare's *Hamlet* (*c*.1601) is the most famous revenge tragedy.

Shakespeare's tragedies are characterised by their variety and freedom from convention, in contrast with those of the slightly later classical French tragedians, Racine and Corneille. Shakespeare's lack of concern for preserving the texts (the plays were collected from a variety of sources by two of his friends, Heminges and Condell) suggests that he regarded them primarily as plays for the stage, and undervalued their literary pretensions. Shakespearean tragedy concentrates on the downfall of powerful men and often illuminates the resulting deterioration of a whole community around them. The protagonists are not necessarily good: *Richard III* (*c*.1592–) is a punitive tragedy in which evil is justly punished. Often the extent to which the tragic fall is deserved is left richly ambiguous: when Lear wails that he is a man 'more sinned against than sinning' we may remark that this is not true at that point in the play. Also in *King Lear* (*c*.1605) when Gloucester reaches the nadir of cynical disbelief in providential justice ('as flies to wanton boys are we to the gods') we know that he is in fact being helped by his son. The relationship between human evil and the justice of fate is at the core of Shakespeare's tragic interests, as are the morality and psychology of his characters: unlike, for example, Sophocles's Oedipus, whose fate is determined before his birth, Shakespeare's protagonists are shown to be responsible for the choices that result in their downfall. This free will is obviously a Christian element which differentiates Renaissance tragedy from Classical models. In order to achieve the great goodness of Christ's crucifixion, which redeems man, the evil of Judas and the Roman soldiers is necessary. The paradoxical interdependence of good and evil in Christian thinking contributes to the special success of tragedy as at genre

tragicomedy a mixture of tragedy and comedy

unities in his *Poetics* (fourth century BC) Aristotle observed that Greek tragedies concentrated on one complete action, or events which took place within a single day and night. These descriptive comments became known as the 'dramatic unities' of action and time (the unity of space was added by later critics), and from the late sixteenth onwards scholars came to regard them as rules for the proper construction of tragedies. From the seventeenth until the nineteenth century French playwrights followed these prescriptions. Following the example of Shakespeare, whose tragedies have multiple actions, and sometimes spread themselves over many years and many different countries, English dramatists tended not to treat the unities as anything but occasional guide-lines

AUTHORS OF THIS NOTE

Lynn and Jeff Wood have written numerous textbooks. They are best known for their ongoing project, *The Cambridge Poetry Workshop*, published by Cambridge University Press. Both have taught in a wide range of 11–18 schools and now work in Cambridge Sixth Form Colleges.

York Notes Advanced

Margaret Atwood
The Handmaid's Tale

Jane Austen
Mansfield Park

Jane Austen
Persuasion

Jane Austen
Pride and Prejudice

Alan Bennett
Talking Heads

William Blake
Songs of Innocence and of Experience

Charlotte Brontë
Jane Eyre

Emily Brontë
Wuthering Heights

Geoffrey Chaucer
The Franklin's Tale

Geoffrey Chaucer
General Prologue to the Canterbury Tales

Geoffrey Chaucer
The Wife of Bath's Prologue and Tale

Joseph Conrad
Heart of Darkness

Charles Dickens
Great Expectations

John Donne
Selected Poems

George Eliot

The Mill on the Floss

F. Scott Fitzgerald
The Great Gatsby

E.M. Forster
A Passage to India

Brian Friel
Translations

Thomas Hardy
The Mayor of Casterbridge

Thomas Hardy
Tess of the d'Urbervilles

Seamus Heaney
Selected Poems from Opened Ground

Nathaniel Hawthorne
The Scarlet Letter

James Joyce
Dubliners

John Keats
Selected Poems

Christopher Marlowe
Doctor Faustus

Arthur Miller
Death of a Salesman

Toni Morrison
Beloved

William Shakespeare
Antony and Cleopatra

William Shakespeare
As You Like It

William Shakespeare

Hamlet

William Shakespeare
King Lear

William Shakespeare
Measure for Measure

William Shakespeare
The Merchant of Venice

William Shakespeare
Much Ado About Nothing

William Shakespeare
Othello

William Shakespeare
Romeo and Juliet

William Shakespeare
The Tempest

William Shakespeare
The Winter's Tale

Mary Shelley
Frankenstein

Alice Walker
The Color Purple

Oscar Wilde
The Importance of Being Earnest

Tennessee Williams
A Streetcar Named Desire

John Webster
The Duchess of Malfi

W.B. Yeats
Selected Poems

OTHER TITLES

GCSE and equivalent levels

Maya Angelou
I Know Why the Caged Bird Sings

Jane Austen
Pride and Prejudice

Alan Ayckbourn
Absent Friends

Elizabeth Barrett Browning
Selected Poems

Robert Bolt
A Man for All Seasons

Harold Brighouse
Hobson's Choice

Charlotte Brontë
Jane Eyre

Emily Brontë
Wuthering Heights

Shelagh Delaney
A Taste of Honey

Charles Dickens
David Copperfield

Charles Dickens
Great Expectations

Charles Dickens
Hard Times

Charles Dickens
Oliver Twist

Roddy Doyle
Paddy Clarke Ha Ha Ha

George Eliot
Silas Marner

George Eliot
The Mill on the Floss

William Golding
Lord of the Flies

Oliver Goldsmith
She Stoops To Conquer

Willis Hall
The Long and the Short and the Tall

Thomas Hardy
Far from the Madding Crowd

Thomas Hardy
The Mayor of Casterbridge

Thomas Hardy
Tess of the d'Urbervilles

Thomas Hardy
The Withered Arm and other Wessex Tales

L.P. Hartley
The Go-Between

Seamus Heaney
Selected Poems

Susan Hill
I'm the King of the Castle

Barry Hines
A Kestrel for a Knave

Louise Lawrence
Children of the Dust

Harper Lee
To Kill a Mockingbird

Laurie Lee
Cider with Rosie

Arthur Miller
The Crucible

Arthur Miller
A View from the Bridge

Robert O'Brien
Z for Zachariah

Frank O'Connor
My Oedipus Complex and other stories

George Orwell
Animal Farm

J.B. Priestley
An Inspector Calls

Willy Russell
Educating Rita

Willy Russell
Our Day Out

J.D. Salinger
The Catcher in the Rye

William Shakespeare
Henry IV Part 1

William Shakespeare
Henry V

William Shakespeare
Julius Caesar

William Shakespeare
Macbeth

William Shakespeare
The Merchant of Venice

William Shakespeare
A Midsummer Night's Dream

William Shakespeare
Much Ado About Nothing

William Shakespeare
Romeo and Juliet

William Shakespeare
The Tempest

William Shakespeare
Twelfth Night

George Bernard Shaw
Pygmalion

Mary Shelley
Frankenstein

R.C. Sherriff
Journey's End

Rukshana Smith
Salt on the snow

John Steinbeck
Of Mice and Men

Robert Louis Stevenson
Dr Jekyll and Mr Hyde

Jonathan Swift
Gulliver's Travels

Robert Swindells
Daz 4 Zoe

Mildred D. Taylor
Roll of Thunder, Hear My Cry

Mark Twain
Huckleberry Finn

James Watson
Talking in Whispers

William Wordsworth
Selected Poems

A Choice of Poets

Mystery Stories of the Nineteenth Century including The Signalman

Nineteenth Century Short Stories

Poetry of the First World War

Six Women Poets

Future titles in the york notes series

Chinua Achebe
Things Fall Apart

Edward Albee
Who's Afraid of Virginia Woolf?

Margaret Atwood
Cat's Eye

Jane Austen
Emma

Jane Austen
Northanger Abbey

Jane Austen
Sense and Sensibility

Samuel Beckett
Waiting for Godot

Robert Browning
Selected Poems

Robert Burns
Selected Poems

Angela Carter
Nights at the Circus

Geoffrey Chaucer
The Merchant's Tale

Geoffrey Chaucer
The Miller's Tale

Geoffrey Chaucer
The Nun's Priest's Tale

Samuel Taylor Coleridge
Selected Poems

Daniel Defoe
Moll Flanders

Daniel Defoe
Robinson Crusoe

Charles Dickens
Bleak House

Charles Dickens
Hard Times

Emily Dickinson
Selected Poems

Carol Ann Duffy
Selected Poems

George Eliot
Middlemarch

T.S. Eliot
The Waste Land

T.S. Eliot
Selected Poems

Henry Fielding
Joseph Andrews

E.M. Forster
Howards End

John Fowles
The French Lieutenant's Woman

Robert Frost
Selected Poems

Elizabeth Gaskell
North and South

Stella Gibbons
Cold Comfort Farm

Graham Greene
Brighton Rock

Thomas Hardy
Jude the Obscure

Thomas Hardy
Selected Poems

Joseph Heller
Catch-22

Homer
The Iliad

Homer
The Odyssey

Gerard Manley Hopkins
Selected Poems

Aldous Huxley
Brave New World

Kazuo Ishiguro
The Remains of the Day

Ben Jonson
The Alchemist

Ben Jonson
Volpone

James Joyce
A Portrait of the Artist as a Young Man

Philip Larkin
Selected Poems

D.H. Lawrence
The Rainbow

D.H. Lawrence
Selected Stories

D.H. Lawrence
Sons and Lovers

D.H. Lawrence
Women in Love

John Milton
Paradise Lost Bks I & II

John Milton
Paradise Lost Bks IV & IX

Thomas More
Utopia

Sean O'Casey
Juno and the Paycock

George Orwell
Nineteen Eighty-four

John Osborne
Look Back in Anger

Wilfred Owen
Selected Poems

Sylvia Plath
Selected Poems

Alexander Pope
Rape of the Lock and other poems

Ruth Prawer Jhabvala
Heat and Dust

Jean Rhys
Wide Sargasso Sea

William Shakespeare
As You Like It

William Shakespeare
Coriolanus

William Shakespeare
Henry IV Pt 1

William Shakespeare
Henry V

William Shakespeare
Julius Caesar

William Shakespeare
Macbeth

William Shakespeare
Measure for Measure

William Shakespeare
A Midsummer Night's Dream

William Shakespeare
Richard II

William Shakespeare
Richard III

William Shakespeare
Sonnets

William Shakespeare
The Taming of the Shrew

William Shakespeare
Twelfth Night

William Shakespeare
The Winter's Tale

George Bernard Shaw
Arms and the Man

George Bernard Shaw
Saint Joan

Muriel Spark
The Prime of Miss Jean Brodie

John Steinbeck
The Grapes of Wrath

John Steinbeck
The Pearl

Tom Stoppard
Arcadia

Tom Stoppard
Rosencrantz and Guildenstern are Dead

Jonathan Swift
Gulliver's Travels and The Modest Proposal

Alfred, Lord Tennyson
Selected Poems

W.M. Thackeray
Vanity Fair

Virgil
The Aeneid

Edith Wharton
The Age of Innocence

Tennessee Williams
Cat on a Hot Tin Roof

Tennessee Williams
The Glass Menagerie

Virginia Woolf
Mrs Dalloway

Virginia Woolf
To the Lighthouse

William Wordsworth
Selected Poems

Metaphysical Poets